# This is Me

## Mrs Hinch

PENGUIN BOOKS

PENGUIN BOOKS

UK | USA | Canada | Ireland | Australia
India | New Zealand | South Africa

Penguin Books is part of the Penguin Random House group of companies
whose addresses can be found at global.penguinrandomhouse.com

First published by Michael Joseph, 2020
This paperback edition published in Penguin Books, 2022
001

Typeset by Jouve (UK), Milton Keynes
Printed and bound in Great Britain by Clays Ltd, Elcograf S.p.A.

The authorized representative in the EEA is Penguin Random House Ireland,
Morrison Chambers, 32 Nassau Street, Dublin D02 YH68

A CIP catalogue record for this book is available from the British Library

ISBN: 978–1–405–94963–7

www.greenpenguin.co.uk

To My Amazing Husband Jamie, My Darling Boys
Ronnie Roo and Henry Hinch, My Family,
My Friends and My Hinchers

# Contents

Welcome to my World      1

1   The Rise of Mrs Hinch      7

2   Back to the Beginning      27

3   Anxiety      57

4   Jamie      83

5   Motherhood      113

6   Body Talk      151

7   The Truth About the Trolls      175

8   Myths and Misconceptions      201

9   The Fame Game      215

10   How the Industry Works      243

11   Growing Our Home      257

12   A Drop into my DMs      277

13   What's Next?      299

All the Best      311

Bonus Chapter: Lennie      315

Acknowledgements      323

# Welcome to my World

I'm sitting here taking some seriously deep breaths because I have so much to tell you that it's hard to even know where to begin!

But let me start by saying hello. I hope you're doing OK and I'm so glad you're here on this journey with me. I'm beyond grateful and constantly blown away by the love and support I feel every day from you guys, and before I go any further, I want to say thank you, from the bottom of my heart. Thank you for allowing me to be me and for helping me to feel proud of who I am.

You have no idea how much you have changed my life and how you have helped me grow as a person. This book is for you.

I'll be honest, this isn't a book I ever thought I would write. This might sound strange seeing as I show you a lot of my life on social media, but I'm actually quite a private person.

I prefer to go through life not making a lot of fuss and

blending into the crowd. I am actually so shy when I don't know people. I've never been comfortable being the centre of attention. I feel physically ill with nerves if I ever have to do any kind of public speaking and there are areas of my life, past and present, that I find difficult to talk about.

So you might be wondering why I've decided to open up more about myself for this memoir. The truth is, I am nervous, and this does feel like a big step for me.

But it feels like the right thing to do and now feels like the right time to do it.

When I wrote *Hinch Yourself Happy* and touched on some quite personal stuff, I had so many messages from people saying how much they could relate to me and my story.

My first book was mainly about Hinching and the beginnings of my Mrs Hinch journey, but it was the little bits about me and my life away from all of that which you guys seemed to love reading about. That really surprised me! I honestly didn't think anyone would be all that interested.

But hearing about the challenges I've faced seemed to strike a chord – people had no idea about some of the things I've been through. There was quite a lot of surprise about my past, especially my gastric band, which helped me lose eight stone but which I've also had a lot of trouble with.

I think some people assumed I was this Essex princess with an always perfect life who had everything land in her lap, which couldn't be further from the truth.

People wanted to know more about the details I'd not yet shared, not feeling ready to go deeper at that time. So, after giving this a lot of thought, I've decided that it's important to answer everyone's questions. It's so hard for me to do that to you all individually because I know now that I will never make it to the bottom of my inbox (as much as I desperately try), but I thought maybe I could get as much of it as I can down in this book . . .

By doing that, I thought I could help other people. Maybe by reading my story you will be able to relate and you won't feel so alone.

As you'll probably already know, I became a mummy last year to Ronnie and so I also wanted the chance to talk openly about motherhood – the highs and the lows – and I hope that by sharing some of my reality, I can show you that we are all in this together. I'm not pretending I know all the answers (I really, *really* don't!), but talking about how we're feeling is so important, and the more we share our experiences, the more we can learn from them and help each other.

On top of all that, I feel like we have got to know one another so well over the last few years and I genuinely see you all as my friends. Maybe some people think that's silly but that's just how I feel! I can chat to you like I do on the phone to my mates.

I see us as very much a two-way relationship and, believe me, you guys are as much of a support to me as you say I am to you.

I have the best followers in the world – it's a real family and one which is open to anyone and everyone who wants to get involved with being part of something amazing. Being a Hincher gives you a real sense of belonging and at the heart of this friendship is kindness, love and understanding. I don't see any nastiness or competition amongst us.

It's never ever been about showing off who's got the biggest and best stuff or the nicest home. No one is better than anyone else. It's a very equal community, which is exactly how it should be. We all just want to help each other; that's what brings us together.

I hope that after reading this book you will know just how much you've done for me. While I've not changed as a person, you guys have helped me to change the way I feel about myself; the way I see myself. The doubters and the haters can make fun of me, but I have over 3 million friends who love and support me and after all these years of self-doubt and low confidence, I've stopped feeling uncomfortable about myself.

I've stopped feeling embarrassed.

If I do something silly or clumsy or daft, you know, just me being typical Soph, I put it on my stories and you guys love it! You laugh with me. You don't judge me – it's never been about using Instagram as a stage or being a performer. It's just always been about being allowed to be me, exactly as I am.

I've always felt that I didn't quite fit in with what was considered 'normal', whether that was because of my weight issues, what happened when I was at school or the anxiety I've suffered with my whole life. I've always been lucky enough to have the most incredible friends and family around me. I've never been one to get involved in going out until the early hours of the morning or wearing short skirts and high heels. That's what everyone else seemed to enjoy doing, but I never did, and I used to wonder if there was something wrong with me because of that.

Which is why finally feeling part of something, accepted and even celebrated just for being me . . . well, that truly is amazing.

Finding something I love doing – being at home Hinching – and realising it's become this really cool thing, blows me away. I've never been a part of anything cool in my life! In so many ways it's been like a fairy tale. For the most part, I'm living my best life with the man I love, our beautiful baby boy Ronnie, handsomes Henry and a successful career I'm excited about every day.

But of course no fairy tale is ever complete without a few bumps in the road. There's a real person behind Mrs Hinch and I have the same hopes, dreams, fears and flaws as anyone else. Reaching the place I am now hasn't been the easiest of journeys.

So, grab a cuppa, light a wax melt, curl up on your sofa with your favourite comfy throw and let's do this like we do everything else: together.

This is me.

# One

# The Rise of Mrs Hinch

It was late in 2019 on a freezing afternoon in Chelmsford when the true scale of how big this Mrs Hinch frenzy had become finally hit me. And, oh my God, did it stop me right in my tracks.

I'd been out signing some stickers on various cleaning bottles in Poundland as part of a fun game for my Hinchers and I was just getting ready to leave when a lady tapped me on the shoulder.

'I just need to say this now because I might not ever see you again,' she said, showing me her NHS lanyard.

She was a GP and she told me that she had a number of patients who'd been able to come off their medication because of watching me on Instagram. She called it the 'Hinch Effect'.

'You are the reason,' she added, 'that they are excited about cleaning their homes. They have something positive to focus on and they've made friends with other Hinchers on social media so they don't feel so alone any more.'

And then she said: 'If we could bottle you, we'd prescribe you.'

I was absolutely lost for words. I mean, literally speechless. I looked at my manager who was with me at the time and she had tears in her eyes. You know when something completely throws you? It was the single most powerful thing anyone has ever said to me and it knocked me sideways.

The GP asked to have a photo with me so she could show her patients the two of us together and I told her to send them my love. And then I stood there, my head still spinning, trying to process what she'd just told me. I don't feel worthy of that sort of praise at all and her words will stay with me forever.

There have been parts of this whole Mrs Hinch experience that have been very challenging for me and I'm going to be open and honest about them in this book. But when I hear a story like that, about the genuinely positive impact that being part of this Hinching community can have on people's lives, everything just lifts and it all makes sense.

I remind myself of these special moments as much as I can to bring home just what's been achieved here. When I sit and look back at everything that's happened over the last two years, it's difficult to wrap my head around. I've lived it and yet I can barely believe it myself at times.

It has been the craziest, most exciting, emotionally charged, overwhelming and completely confusing adventure, and parts of my life have changed beyond anything I recognise, and could have ever imagined.

Going from just a few friends and family to over 3 million followers, seeing myself in cartoon form all over the supermarkets as the face of Procter & Gamble and shooting for the cover of the *Daily Mail*'s *You* magazine (Me! A cover girl!) are just a few of the things I'm still trying to process.

But without a doubt, it's the response to my books that has blown me away most of all. Seeing my first book, *Hinch Yourself Happy*, on *The Sunday Times* Bestseller List higher up the charts than people like Elton John and Michelle Obama, whose names give me actual goose bumps, was probably the biggest 'pinch-me' moment so far. Pass me the smelling salts because I'm still in a state of absolute shock about that!

And when *The Activity Journal* also went to number one, followed by my *Little Book of Lists* on pre-orders alone, it meant that for a few weeks at the start of this year, I had three books in the top 10. What the actual hell?!

You guys came out to support me in such huge numbers for the *Hinch Yourself Happy* book tour in 2019 that when I did the signing event at Lakeside in Essex, it took me three attempts to walk through the double doors because I needed to take a few deep breaths when I saw the size of the queue wrapping around the mall. It's one thing seeing the mind-blowing follower numbers on the screen but it's quite something else to see how that looks in real life, and that was the first time I'd seen physical proof of what was happening here.

As I walked down the line, it blew my mind. I was so overcome that I started crying and everyone collectively 'ahhed', which set me off even more.

The turnout was the same wherever we went, rain or shine, and I remember thinking I couldn't believe that the Hinchers in Liverpool had waited outside in the freezing cold for me. We were so worried about everyone that Jamie went into Primark to get blankets for those queueing so they could keep warm while they waited in line.

Going on to *The Chris Evans Breakfast Show* on Virgin Radio last April was another big moment for me. Obviously he's one of the biggest and most famous radio DJs in the country and I was so, so nervous about doing live radio.

Chris is someone I've watched for years on the telly and I was shocked that he actually even knew who I was. I got so starstruck, it was embarrassing. I was physically shaking but he was brilliant at settling my nerves.

He said: 'Don't worry, we're only having a chat. I'd never put you on the spot!'

He was so funny and cheerful and he put me right at ease. All my Hinchers were phoning in and sending lovely messages during the show and that really helped me through it. And when I went on the show for the second time last October, Chris welcomed me like an old mate and I was a lot less panicky.

'How have you been?' he asked. 'I saw you cleaning your loo the other day!' And that made me laugh.

Don't get me wrong, though, I was still way out of my comfort zone, and I'm not sure I'll ever get used to this new, crazy life in the spotlight. I'm both flattered and amazed that the likes of *Loose Women* and *This Morning* – shows I've watched and loved for years – have invited me on to talk about my book.

I was so happy to be given the opportunity to do that, because *Hinch Yourself Happy* was something I worked hard on and am very proud of, so of course I wanted to tell people about it.

It was exciting meeting the *Loose Women* gang (love 'em!) and Holly and Phil are just as lovely in real life as you'd expect, but honestly, I'm much happier watching those shows in the comfort of my own home on the sofa than being on them!

Being interviewed on the telly is still a bizarre experience for me because I don't see myself as a celebrity in any way. I actually feel safer on radio than I do on TV because you're behind the mic where no one sees you. Radio is definitely more my cup of tea.

It's embarrassing how nervous I get when I'm introduced to celebrities. I will never be the sort of person who can play it cool. It's just not in my nature.

I went to FriendsFest in London with my sister and niece, a brilliant event to celebrate *Friends*, which is one of my most favourite programmes ever. All of the *EastEnders* lot were there as well and Louisa Lytton and Danielle Harold who play Ruby and Lola came up to us and asked ME to have a picture with them! How funny is that? It should be the other way around!

Actually, one of the most ludicrous things to happen in all this was when I was watching an episode of *EastEnders* and Robbie Jackson said he was 'Hinching' his kitchen.

I nearly choked on my custard cream!

Jamie said: 'Did you just hear what I just heard?' And we had to rewind it and watch again to make sure. Madness. And then it happened again when I got a cheeky mention in *Coronation Street*! I've grown up watching these programmes on the telly. It blows my mind!

Earlier this year, my all-time celebrity crush when I was growing up, Lee Ryan from Blue, got in touch after he saw me refer to him on my stories. I didn't even realise he followed me! If I'd been able to tell eleven-year-old me that one day Lee Ryan would know my name, she'd have most likely burst on the spot.

You probably saw from my stories what it reduced me to even as a (relatively) sane adult – a quivering, dribbling mess! See, I told you I couldn't act cool to save my life.

My most starstruck moment, though, came when Marie Kondo – the goddess of decluttering, organising and tidying – DM'd me. Actual Marie Kondo.

I'd tagged her in a story of me folding Jamie's underpants and putting them away in the drawer (the glamour!) and she replied!

No joke, I nearly fainted. I was running about the house like: 'Oh my gosh, Marie is my best mate!' That was Insta goals for me, right there! She's not been back in touch since, mind. But I live in eternal hope.

While there have been incredible highs and I'm so thankful for every one of them, I do want to be totally honest with you guys. The truth is, my life has been turned on its head and I've had to get used to a 'new normal', which hasn't been easy. And I'm not quite there yet.

I don't think it will ever really make sense to me because not one bit of this was planned. I've barely even left my house apart from the occasional trip to B&M and yet everything has changed!

Why me? I truly don't know. It's not the way I look because I didn't show myself for the longest time and even now I cover myself up and mostly hide behind a filter on Instagram. It's not because I have a huge mansion dripping with designer furniture – because I don't. It's not because I've got the perfect body or amazing make-up skills, or even any particular talent.

So what on earth is it? I really wish I knew.

When I started my @mrshinchhome account back in 2018, it was so I could share little updates with friends and family of things I'd bought to make our new house look nice. It was more for me than anything else, a bit like an online scrapbook and somewhere I could document everything, swap ideas and get some inspiration.

I soon realised that Instagram was a really positive,

supportive place and I started making connections with various other interiors accounts.

I became Insta friends with some lovely people; we'd comment on and like each other's posts and I learned about things like using hashtags and follow trains in order to get my posts seen by more people.

By April 2018 and after only a month, I'd somehow reached 1,000 followers and was really enjoying being on there each day, posting my pictures and seeing my account grow.

I'd started posting what I thought were nothing more than silly videos on my stories of me cleaning to my favourite tunes, but they seemed to be really popular. People also found it hilarious that I named all my cloths (big up Minkeh, Dave, Kermit, Pinkeh and the rest of the family!) which made me smile because it's just something I've always done but never admitted to out loud. I thought people would think I was crazy for it, but they loved it.

For some reason it was a story of me shining my sink one night that caused the biggest reaction. I used Cif – or, rather, Cliff as I like to call him – teamed with Buddy, gave them a banging R&B backing track, as you know I love to do, and suddenly my inbox was flooded with DMs. It's so funny what gets people going, isn't it?

After that, cleaning my sink and putting my cloths to bed became a nightly routine and my following continued going up at the most insane rate. Like, tens of thousands of people, every day.

I remember being a bit stunned by it all and saying to my mum: 'Mum, I'm getting all of these followers; they're just going up and up. And it isn't showing any signs of slowing down. And I have no idea why.'

My mum, bless her, isn't clued up about social media in the slightest so it was even more baffling to her.

She said: 'What have you done here, Soph?'

'I dunno, Mum! I've just been shining my sink!'

My mum says that 'I was just . . .' has been my catch-phrase my whole life, and whenever I say it, she thinks: 'Oh God, here we go . . .' because it usually means I've accidentally caused some sort of drama.

She looked at me, smiled and shook her head and said: 'Only you, Soph. Only you.'

I think it was when my beloved Minky cloths sold out around the world after I'd used them to Hinch my kitchen that I was like: 'Hold on a minute, something seriously weird is happening here.'

There was a time when you couldn't get Minkys any-where apart from some devious traders on Amazon who were taking the mickey out of the situation and whacking the usual price up from £2.49 to thirty quid a pop.

I told my followers to hang on, not to fall for the con artists and that Minky would be getting more out as soon as they could. That was a position I didn't think I'd ever find myself in.

From there, you could say it snowballed although it felt more like an avalanche, if I'm honest. It was unstoppable.

Word travels fast on Instagram and I was suddenly gaining 50,000 followers a day. The numbers were out of this world.

People with big followings were sharing my posts and stories and then the press started to pick up on me as well. When I hit the mainstream media, the attention moved up another level and after that, there was no going back.

I can't explain why it happened and if you asked me to go back and repeat it, I couldn't. But it all came together and just seemed to explode.

I started getting emails from brands and companies saying they'd like to work with me, because they'd seen products like the Minky cloth and my Vileda mop (Vera to her friends), which I used and recommended, selling so well. But while I was interested to hear more about these opportunities that were becoming available to me, I had no idea what to do with all of these requests and offers. I'd only ever worked in sales and then trained as a hairdresser, so this was all completely alien to me – I didn't even know being an influencer was a job and yet I found myself being referred to as one!

I was completely clueless in this new world and it didn't take long before I felt like I was drowning.

I desperately needed some help to handle all of it and so one of my good friends, who knows way more about this kind of stuff than I do, suggested I looked into accepting one of the offers I'd received to work alongside a management company who deal with all of these things for you. Here's the thing: I didn't actually need help finding the opportunities because they were already there. Amazingly, my account had already generated those. But I did need help with the volume that was coming in, handling those conversations and the legal and the business side that comes with them, which I had absolutely no clue about.

We worked our way through the offers I'd received from agencies, and even set up and had phone meetings with a few of them to get a feel for what they were about. I remember feeling so lucky to be in a position where I could choose the right fit. But for some reason, none of them felt like they were 'the one' for me. What I didn't realise was that, in the background, my friend had put some feelers out and told an agency called Gleam about me and my account. They had the reputation of being the best of the best when it came to looking after social media influencers.

It was the summer of 2018 by then and I was already on a few hundred thousand followers, and one of the girls at Gleam, who ended up being my manager, happened to be a Hincher herself and had seen first-hand how my follower count was rocketing.

She went to her boss and said they should definitely set up a meeting with me and that she would make the time to take me on, even though their roster was full and they weren't taking on any new clients. I met up with the team shortly after at their offices in London, and the rest is history, as they say.

My Instagram has grown quite considerably since then and especially since hitting the million mark in October 2018.

It's not just cleaning any more. Let's face it, I've never claimed to be a professional cleaner. I just like my house to look nice and I release a lot of stress and nerves keeping myself busy in my home.

In the last two years I've got married to Jamie and become a mum to our Ronnie, and over the weeks and months, it became clear that my Hinchers also liked hearing about what was going on in our lives as well as seeing our house, and the Hinching, of course. Which actually came as a huge relief to me. We've all built this friendship which might sound strange to some, because I've never met most of you – and there are so many of you! But I just know you guys feel the same.

Opening up a bit more online about myself and Hinch family life happened very naturally. It wasn't something that I consciously set out to do. There was no masterplan or super strategy in place, regardless of what the cynics think . . .

I guess this change started around the wedding, when Jamie was coming on to my stories more often and people were asking questions about him. Loads of you wanted to know if he Hinched as well and so one day as a little joke, I gave him a Hinch List to do on my stories. You lot loved him!

Jamie is a really funny man. He makes people laugh with his banter but he's also very kind and caring and my followers aren't daft – you guys can hear support and love through a story. You feel it too. And I think that's why you have stuck with us as a family.

You've seen us get married, have a baby and grow our home, and you've supported us through every little step of that journey. We have a community here and we're all invested in each other, aren't we? So if I was to slow down Hinching tomorrow, obviously I'd lose some of my followers, but I think the majority would stay with us.

If anything, I hope my journey will send a message to the younger girls and boys out there that you don't need to be some glam designer-dripping influencer to get respect and love from people. Often just being yourself works best, and that's enough, even if that means you're in your slippers all day and pining your toilet.

I'm not posing on a luxury yacht, head to toe in Dior, bum out and boobs pushed up. You'll find me sitting here on the sofa.

I've never pretended to be anything I'm not. There was an interview I did once on one of the posh radio stations and they ridiculed me, saying: 'You shouldn't be as big as you are for what you do, you're taking women back to the Dark Ages.'

What's that all about exactly? They made me feel terrible for just being myself and doing what I love. People wouldn't follow me if they didn't want to and I've never said I was doing anything revolutionary. I'm just a girl who likes to keep her house right and have a bit of fun while I do it. Every woman has the right to do whatever it is she chooses; whether that's being the CEO of a company, a stay at home mum, or both! And actually, you'll be surprised at how many of my Hinchers are men!

As Mrs Hinch has blown up, one of the ways I've tried to keep myself hidden from the limelight I'm so uncomfortable with is by using what's become known as the Gretel filter on my stories. Most of the time when I speak face-to-face with the camera, I stick Gretel on and she banters away quite happily in a way I don't think I ever could as Sophie.

People think I use it to try and be funny (and I know she can be hilarious, bless her) but the reasons behind me using Gretel go much deeper than that. I would actually struggle to continue on Instagram without her. She is my alter ego – my safety blanket – and she allows me to speak freely. It's hard to explain, but if anyone pulls her apart, it doesn't matter as much to me, because it's technically not me.

She feels very separate and she gives me the confidence I need to carry on with my account.

Not that I'd ever dare compare myself to Queen Bey, but I suppose it's a bit like when Beyoncé becomes Sasha Fierce on stage or when Paul O'Grady dressed up as Lily Savage. They're an extension of their personality and they say and do things they wouldn't feel able to themselves. Gretel is that for me.

Gosh, I do love her. Some days I look at her and wish she was my friend! I watch her and think: 'Oh my God, we have so much in common!'

I'm fully aware that sounds completely mad, by the way.

It's the same with the P&G Mrs Hinch cartoons. They wanted my photo everywhere in the shops to advertise the products I promote, but I just couldn't have done that. I would have been mortified going into B&M and seeing myself plastered all over the cleaning aisle.

So I suggested making a fun cartoon of me instead. Again, it's not me, there's a point of separation, and that makes me feel safe.

Putting my whole self out there isn't something I can be OK with. I've tried to convince myself to go to certain events but when it comes to the crunch, I just can't do it. I turned down an invite to the Baftas this year because doing the red carpet doesn't feel right to me. In fact, I'm cold sweating now just thinking about it! I feel physically sick.

Apparently me and Jamie would have been sat at a table next to Brad Pitt (although he later pulled out anyway – all the best, Brad!) but I'd much rather curl up on my sofa and watch all the glamour and beautiful dresses from the comfort of my living room.

Give me a dressing gown over a ballgown any day! Although I've always wanted another excuse to wear an incredible dress, hence the front cover of my book. I was talking to my mum about what she thought I should do for the shoot, and she said: 'Wear the most amazing dress you can find, Soph, but don't even leave the house!' So I've done exactly that. Both of my dreams captured in one!

I'm not doing any of this for the fame or the glory – I've only recently actually sat down and thought about what my long-term goal with all of this is, because I just never expected it. I think ultimately I'd like what anyone would love for their family – stability. And so if I can build a trusted brand that will provide for my family's future, then what an incredible position to be in. But I do love being able to use what is a fortunate position to make a difference. I'm incredibly lucky to be here and I feel that it's important to give something back.

A huge milestone for me in my Hinch journey was getting involved with Place2Be, which is a children's mental health charity. I wanted to launch a range of loungewear – my favourite kind of clothing – and have 100 per cent of the profits go to a charity who would really benefit from the money.

Place2Be was perfect. They do fantastic work with vulnerable young people; providing counselling, mental health support and training and, having been subject to nastiness when I was at school, this is something I feel so incredibly passionate about.

We launched the range in the autumn of 2019 and, Hinchers, I never doubted you. While I hoped it would sell well because you guys always support me, I didn't bank on it selling out within an hour of me putting the swipe-up on my stories. It was incredible and I'm so proud of what we achieved together there.

The money you all spent will help thousands of children and allow the fantastic staff to keep on doing what they do. I'd love to do something like that as often as I can, at least every year for a different charity each time. I'm really looking forward to connecting with an animal charity next, so I'll keep you all posted on that.

I'd much rather do things like that which will help other people.

I'm the same when it comes to spending money. I know I'm paid very well by the brands I work with and I'm more financially comfortable than I ever expected to be at the age of thirty, but I've never been a big spender and that hasn't changed. I prefer to buy things for my family and friends instead.

One thing I've loved to see coming out of all this has been the 'cleanfluencer' revolution. People have fallen in love with Hinching and think they'd quite like to have a go themselves, which is amazing.

I can honestly say I don't feel the slightest bit competitive with any of it. It actually makes me smile and if people can get a buzz from it like I have, then that's fantastic to me. Everyone has a home to share, everyone has a toilet to clean, and I firmly believe there is room for us all.

I'm definitely not the expert on all things cleaning and there is plenty I learn from lots of other amazing people on Instagram.

I'm very open if and when I get ideas from others. My 'flip your lids' post, where I showed how you could save space in your cupboards by stacking your pans on top of each other with the lids upside down, caused a social media meltdown. I mean, it's actually genius, right?!

But I made it clear that it had come from a follower and it wasn't my original idea. I tried it, loved it and so I shared it. I'm not 'stealing' someone's saucepan hack.

I *will* claim the word Hinching, though, because that's definitely mine!

The incredible thing about Instagram is that there is something for everyone and so if you want to use potato peel to clean your cutlery or a lemon to clean your oven, then while that's not necessarily my thing, there are people you can follow who will show you how.

I'm not interested in competing with anyone and besides (whisper it!), I don't actually mind if my account doesn't get any bigger. My followers continue to climb and I'm grateful for each and every one, but this has never been about numbers to me.

I'm being who I am, doing what I need to do and cracking on, and it's working, which is an amazing position to be in. But if anything, I'd like things to slow down eventually so I can start building a future for Ronnie and any other children that, with any luck, we go on to have.

It's been the wildest of rides so far and the love and support I get from my Hinchers, which is nothing short of phenomenal, has carried me through the highs and the lows.

Where do we go from here?

Guys, I couldn't have dreamt any of this so far, so I'm the last person who should start making predictions now!

So we'll see. It's with a mixture of excitement and more than a little nervousness that I'm looking forward to finding out exactly what's in store next for Mrs Hinch.

# Two

## Back to the Beginning

My mum told me recently that her and my dad always knew something out of the ordinary was going to happen to me.

They weren't sure what it was going to be, but they didn't ever think I was headed for your straightforward, run-of-the-mill kind of life. I was messy, scatty, clumsy and impulsive as a child. I always needed a lot of reassurance, and some of the most everyday, seemingly low-risk events would often end in some sort of drama.

I wouldn't just go out on my roller skates, fall down and graze my knees like the other kids. Instead, I'd somehow manage to crash-land flat on my face and break my wrist. That sort of thing. Clearly I've never done things by halves.

Mum and Dad knew from day one they were going to have their hands full, and Mum says they'd often look at each other and ask: 'What have we let ourselves in for here?'

I was born on 16 February 1990 at Basildon Hospital and grew up on a tight-knit little cul-de-sac that was known as 'The Close', where everyone was in and out of each other's houses and chatting over cups of tea and coffee.

There was a lot of warmth and friendliness between us all as neighbours and it felt like a very safe place to be – there were always loads of kids on the street and we used to be outside all day long, riding our bikes, pushing our dolls around in their prams, collecting berries from the bushes and trees and making birds' nests from the freshly cut grass in the fields.

I'd get into bed at the end of each day (normally with bruised legs from various tumbles), shattered from all the playing outside in the fresh air. If it sounds almost too good to be true, that's because it was, and it's the kind of freedom and joy that I hope I can give to Ronnie one day.

I'd love for him to be outside, running through fields and having fun, making a mess and getting dirty in the garden.

My dad originally comes from County Durham where he used to work in the mines. He has worked his way up to be a Project Director at a large construction engineering company and I'm so proud of him and what he's achieved in life.

My mum stayed at home to look after me and my sister, although once we were older, she went to work in a florist and stayed there for more than twenty years. I love that she carved out a career for herself and always had that independence.

We weren't 'rich' by any means while we were growing up, but Mum and Dad made sure we wanted for nothing and there was always a massive amount of love in our home.

I remember my absolute pride and joy was my toy kitchen with the Velcro food you could pretend to cut up. It even had a little sink! Maybe that was a sign of things to come!

I also had a little washing line with pegs so I could hang my dolls' clothes out. In the summer I'd have my kitchen and washing line all set up in the garden, with the sink filled with suds. Absolute heaven!

Mum used to take me and my sister horse riding on a Saturday and we loved it so much that when we got home we'd pretend our bikes were ponies called Penny and Coco.

We'd put our bathrobe belts on them, which we'd use as toy reins; the driveway would double up as the stables and we'd wash them down with the hosepipe and tie them up – not that they were going anywhere, obviously! Imaginary play is so important for kids and definitely something I'm going to encourage with Ronnie.

But I didn't half get into some scrapes. One day when I was seven, I was playing hairdressers with my friend and decided to cut myself a fringe, as you do.

Unfortunately, I held the hair between my fingers and cut above them rather than below and so ended up with a huge step right in the middle of my forehead. I knew I was due home for dinner and I was dreading having to face my mum.

She opened the door to let me in and burst into tears.

'What have you done, Sophie?' she cried, looking at my butchered fringe.

For months I had to wear a hairband to school while the missing clump grew back in, but the random tufts would keep spiking up and I remember Mum trying to pin them down with a ton of hairspray each morning.

That was me all over, though. Act now, think later.

Like the time I was six and walked out of school and all the way home on my own. When my mum came to pick me up from after-school club and I wasn't there, she was frantic and my sister went running off trying to find me. The fifteen-minute walk home involved crossing busy roads and going down a cycle track and through the woods, and I remember thinking: 'Watch out for the cars, Soph.' Terrible!

I'd strolled out the gates without a second thought, and although I got home in one piece, thank God, I arrived at an empty house because they were all out looking for me. It still didn't cross my mind what I'd done, and I just went to knock on my friend's door who lived across the road. I stayed there until my mum arrived home, furious with me for what I'd done.

I have no idea why I did that. Maybe I just didn't fancy after-school club that day and thought I'd get home earlier. Who even knows?

Probably the most extreme example of my careless streak was when I set fire to the house with all my family in it. Yes, really.

My mum had this pink silk bag in her bedroom drawer that I knew was strictly out of bounds. She'd always say to keep out of her drawers and definitely *never* to go into that bag.

Sorry, Mum, but that was like a red rag to a bull for me and so one evening – I must have been about seven – I crept into the room and found this bag. It was full of lighters and matches.

I had a piece of paper in my hand which I managed to light, and I remember the flame flickering its way down towards my fingers. Obviously, it started to burn, so I dropped the paper to the floor where the flames caught the valance sheet along the bottom of the bed before flicking their way over to the curtains. Oops!

I completely panicked, but instead of running downstairs to tell my mum and dad that the house was burning down, I ran out the front door and across the road to my friend's again.

I knocked on the door and her mum answered.

'Sophie, what's going on?'

'My house is on fire!'

It was probably the last thing the poor woman expected

me to say. She ran back across with me and within minutes there were fire engines on the scene, ambulances,
the lot. Everyone was fine, thank God, but there was a
hell of a lot of damage to the guest bedroom and the
landing that took a long time to repair.

And I'd literally left them in the house! My sister was
fast asleep! I mean, who does that?

Gosh, I got the telling-off of my life after that, although
it was overridden with relief that everyone was OK. The
whole story even ended up in the local newspaper, would
you believe? I remember my mum saying: 'As if our
Sophie is in the paper!'

And she also said that for some reason she knew it
wouldn't be the last time I'd make the headlines ...
Spooky, right?

I had my own bedroom and it was a lovely size with all
the toys I could wish for, and everything had its own box,
basket and place. My love for organisation obviously
started very young!

I adored my Barbies and I remember setting up little
homes for them on the landing, using random things for
furniture like cotton reels as tables and chairs. I'd have
little bits of my mum's fabric off-cuts which I'd make into
rugs and blankets for them.

My mum was always very creative so she would get the
sewing machine out and make these lovely little cushions
for my dolls to match the bedding.

We would go to the charity shops and buy real baby

clothes so I could dress my dolls, which worked out much cheaper than buying the official merchandise for the likes of Baby Born and Baby Annabell. We'd go down the high street and get the cutest outfit, all for just 50p.

I was normally very good at taking care of my toys, but one day I decided all my Barbies needed a haircut. So on the same sort of thoughtless whim that has always got me into trouble, I chopped off all their beautiful blonde hair with a pair of kitchen scissors.

I regretted it immediately but my mum said I'd made my bed and so now I needed to lie in it.

'Your Barbies have no hair now,' she said. 'Deal with it.'

In other words, there's no way we're buying you a load of replacement Barbies. Lesson learned.

My sister is four years older than me and altogether the more mature, cooler sister. I always idolised her growing up and thought she was amazing, and I still do.

I was never normally allowed to go in her room, although on the odd occasion she'd let me come in while she was getting ready to go out as long as I sat on the bed, kept quiet and didn't touch anything.

Of course I followed her rules – I was just so excited to be let in. I thought she was so grown up and mature and I longed to be like her, but she just saw me as her annoying little sister. But I always knew she loved me really.

Whenever she had friends round, I was desperate to hang out with them, but they had no interest in her little sister coming along and cramping their style. They'd be blasting out All Saints on the CD player and I'd knock on the door and ask if I could come in and play with them.

And the reply would always be: 'No, go away!' and I'd be so, so disappointed.

I remember one time when I was about seven or eight, my mum shouted up to my sister from downstairs and demanded she let me play with them for five minutes before my bath.

She opened the door and said: 'OK, right, we're playing shops and you can be the security guard.'

Then she shut the door again and made me stand outside on the landing on my own. I was so grateful to be involved that I just went along with it.

I was going to be the best security guard ever. Whenever any of them came out of the shop, my role would begin.

And I stood there waiting. And waiting.

Any minute now. Surely someone was going to come out eventually?

But they never did.

In fact, I was there for so long that I dropped off and Mum came upstairs and found me asleep outside my sister's bedroom door.

'Samantha!' she said. 'Your sister is asleep!'

We still laugh about it now and Sam says she can't believe she did that to me.

We did get on, though, and are incredibly close today as

adults. I'm so grateful for the strong bond that we have. I love her so much and I don't know what I'd do without her.

She loved Westlife and we used to make up dance routines to the songs and then make Mum and Dad sit on the sofa and watch our show. Lucky them!

We always expected a very enthusiastic clapping session at the end.

I loved pop music too and was obsessed with the Spice Girls, S Club 7, 5ive and Blue. I was the Spice Girls' number one fan and had every single piece of merchandise you could imagine – mugs, T-shirts, stickers, everything – and it was mainly their posters that I had on my wall.

Oh, and a huge one of Blue. As you know, I had a terrible crush on Lee Ryan! I just thought he had the most amazing voice and I used to imagine he was singing only to me. To think that he saw me raving about him on my stories and that he follows me now is just insane. Can't believe it.

I also developed a massive appreciation for Michael Bolton from being around my mum, who used to play him on repeat. I know every word to every song and I have absolutely no shame in admitting that I used to fancy the pants off of him!

My love of music and singing meant that I wanted a disco party for my birthday every year. My mum would hire out the village hall and I'd invite the whole class, handing out the little paper invitations – these days most kids are invited by Facebook or the class WhatsApp group, but

I used to love my invites going out in their little envelopes. I would have a face painter and karaoke machine every year – they were my two birthday party must-haves. And I'd belt out Céline Dion's 'Think Twice', doing the iconic 'no, no, no, no!' line with my face painted as a Dalmatian.

What must I have looked like? I was in my element, though.

My cake would always be a chocolate caterpillar and as the birthday girl I'd be allowed the face – the best bit, hands down. That was easily my highlight of the day. Possibly even the whole year!

I know there's this modern trend for these showstopper cakes nowadays, but back then, to me, there was nothing much better in life than a chocolate caterpillar.

I never wanted anything particularly flash for birthdays or Christmas. It never even crossed my mind. I didn't ask for expensive trainers – mine were always unbranded, had a Velcro fastening, were bought from Shoe Zone and the more the soles lit up with obnoxious flashing lights, the better. Happy days!

On the subject of discos, my outfits to the school discos over the years were something else. I recently found a photo of me wearing a deep emerald-green velvet top with a silky green skirt, frilly socks and – wait for it – Timberland boots. What is *that* about? I have no idea what was going on there but at the time I thought I was the bee's knees.

I also had a little brown leather handbag to match the

boots that had my 50p in it so I could get a paper bag of mix-up sweets.

It's all different now. I took my niece to her school disco recently and most of the kids were standing around on their phones taking selfies. And there was no dancing!

Isn't it a shame? Wouldn't it be amazing if the next generation of kids just had old-style Nokias and only used them for keeping in touch and to play the odd game of Snake?

Being born in 1990 I've always been very aware of when the world shifted and childhoods seemed to change. I feel like I grew up right in between the before and after of mobile phones so I've got a very clear view on it and can see a lot of positives but also a fair few negatives.

All my mates had a mobile before me but my mum and dad were insistent I had to wait and I remember finally getting one for Christmas when I was twelve. It was a pay-as-you-go Motorola that flipped up and to me it was the best thing ever.

Even then I was only allowed it if I went out, and Mum would put just £10 a month credit on it so I couldn't go crazy.

I'd send texts to my friends; really deep and meaningful chats like: 'wot ru doin?' It felt amazing just doing the textspeak! I thought I was so cool.

For some reason, I never really got into reading books. I remember reading a story called *The Ghost Dog* when I was about ten and also *The Lion, the Witch and the Wardrobe* by C. S. Lewis as a teenager – the inspiration for my Narnia, of course, my cupboard of dreams where I keep all my Hinching supplies.

It's funny now to think that dogs and Narnia turned out to be two very important parts of my life.

I did like being read to, though, and when I was younger, my dad would read to me every night. Because he's from the North East, I'd go into school and read out loud to the teacher in the same Durham accent that he read to me in!

My favourite was called *The Magic Toyshop*, which was about toys that came to life at night. Me and my mum have searched high and low for that book because I really wanted to pass it on to Ronnie, but we've not been able to find my original copy anywhere. I eventually tracked a copy down on eBay and reading it to Ronnie now gives me such warm, fuzzy feelings. I still remember it off by heart.

I was never in danger of being a bookworm, but I did like magazines. There was a row of little shops near us which was known locally as the Top Shops, with a bakery, a hairdresser's, a chippy and a newsagent, and I remember going to spend my pocket money each week on *Girl Talk* magazine.

I was buzzing on life if there was a free piece of make-up attached to the cover. I enjoyed the toy reviews, the step-by-step hairstyle tutorials and the little features on the people I used to watch on the telly like *Sabrina the Teenage Witch* and *Saved by the Bell*, two programmes I watched religiously.

As I moved through the years at primary school, my confidence grew, but I was always very much a mummy's girl and loved nothing more than coming home.

To start with I would go home for my lunch, but once I was up to staying at school for the whole day, my mum would make me packed lunches with a cheese and Marmite sandwich, a yoghurt, a packet of crisps, a Club bar and a little red box of raisins alongside a little note saying things like: 'Only three hours to go' (because it would be midday and only three hours until home time) or 'It's a good day, kidda.'

Kidda. That's her nickname for me. My dad calls me Bubberloo. Yep, even now!

I needed to feel close to my mum even when we were apart. I had a little cotton handkerchief with a peach border that was sprayed with her 1881 perfume and I'd keep it up my sleeve so I could smell it during class. She'd spray it fresh every few days and it was a huge source of comfort for me while we were separated during the day. It made me feel safe. If I could smell my mum, I was OK.

It's funny, because familiar smells have carried on being very calming for me throughout my life and I use them to relate back and be reminded of things.

People think I'm strange for always using the same products, but if I find something I love I will use it forever. I don't care what money I'm offered to promote other items; I will stick to what I know if it works well because it makes me feel comforted and safe.

That's why I'm so attached to things like Lenor's Spring Awakening and Zoflora's Springtime (which they actually discontinued but brought back earlier this year around the time I mentioned how much I missed it – I couldn't believe it).

When I unscrewed the cap of that new bottle of Springtime, I felt my whole body relax. I feel so much better now I've got it back in the house.

They've even brought it out in a bottle which is four times the size of the normal one – thanks, guys! – so thankfully I don't think I'll ever run low on it again.

I could be blindfolded and taken into five different houses and I'd know as soon as I was in mine just by the scent. In fact, I'd even know what room I was in because I know how each one smells.

Weirdly, I used to love the smell of pine although that's changed slightly since I had Ronnie and I have no idea why. Don't get me wrong, I still love pining my toilet, but I'm no longer hunting down anything pine like I used to. Before Ronnie came along, I never used to be much of a citrus lover either, but I really don't mind it now. Strange, isn't it?

I think smells can remind us of so much and our sense of it is really underrated.

Years later I would have a similar handkerchief to the one I had from my mum made for my dad on my wedding day, embroidered with the date and sprayed with my perfume. He wept when I gave it to him. Unfortunately, he lost it at the wedding and he was so upset. I phoned the venue but they couldn't find it. So I ordered him a new one – it was an eBayer – and I told him a little white lie that they'd found the original. He was over the moon and will probably laugh his head off when he reads the truth in this book!

By the time I got to Year 6 – the final year before secondary – I was having the best time of my whole school life. We were the oldest kids in the school and I suddenly felt so grown up.

I remember the first boy I fancied was called Daniel and I hope to God he doesn't ever read this. We were on our end-of-year trip staying in static caravans in Bude, North Cornwall; boys in one caravan, girls in the other, and we'd all been allowed to bring £10 spending money.

Daniel went to the shop and blew the lot on a blue beanie bear which said 'Sophie' on it and then came into my caravan, got down on one knee and asked me to be his girlfriend! It was so sweet but I nearly died.

Part of me was thrilled because I thought he was lovely but it also made me nervous because I was only eleven and didn't really want a boyfriend. I spent the next three days worrying about that and the fact I had this bear and that his mum was going to tell me off because he'd spent his whole tenner on me.

Luckily, it turned out that what went on in Bude stayed in Bude, because when we got back to school, it was like none of it had ever happened. In fact, it was never mentioned again. Phew!

Shortly before I started secondary school, a close family member on my mum's side became very ill with pancreatitis. She went on to make a full recovery and is as fit as a fiddle now, but it meant my mum, as the eldest and very much the mother figure on her side of the family, had to travel back to London a lot to look after her.

It was the first time we'd spent long spells apart. My mum had never missed anything before then – school assemblies, first days, parents' evenings, she'd been there for everything – but she wasn't able to be there for my first day of secondary school, which was very sad for all of us.

Dad was around but obviously he had to go to work, so my sister basically took charge and she became like a surrogate mother to me for a while. I was anxious on my first day, even more so without Mum there, but Sam, bless her, got my bag packed, put my hair up and walked me in. She even sprayed me with a little squirt of her perfume before she said goodbye.

I remember Dad bought me my new school shoes, but we found out the night before the first day of term that they were the wrong size and so I had to wear trainers for a few days instead. Normally, Mum would have had it all organised in good time and had me wear the new shoes in around the house for a few days before the start of term.

I'm sure to a lot of kids, this would have been no drama at all. But I was upset about it because not having exactly the right footwear might have made me stand out and these were the sorts of things I would worry about as a child. I'm exactly the same today as I was back then and can't bear it if I don't blend into the crowd. This is one of the reasons why I don't like wearing heels. It's always been a dream of mine to wear high heels, high wedges, and for them to make that noise when they hit a hard floor. You know the noise I mean? I feel like I've waited twenty plus years to feel comfortable in high shoes and it's never happened, and I realise now, it never will. It's one thing I've really struggled with. I wish so much I could accept and learn to embrace my height.

Poor Dad took a photo of me and Sam walking to school together on that first day and when he showed it to my mum, she said straightaway: 'Why is Sophie wearing trainers?!'

It was the first thing she noticed and she was horrified! Nothing gets past my mum.

My sister would walk me to school every morning and also meet me afterwards to go home together and always made sure that there was stuff I liked in for dinner. Looking back, she was still only fifteen herself, so it was pretty incredible what she did for me over the few months that Mum was back and forth to London, and we got into a little routine that brought us very close. I became used to sharing everything about my day with her.

Starting secondary school was a big deal for so many reasons, but getting a ring-bound planner and a key to my own locker were the two things I was most looking forward to. That's literally all I wanted in life.

It's actually quite embarrassing how excited I was to get my planner, but I've always loved stationery and when I was little I played post offices endlessly with my highlighter pens and favourite hole punch. It's actually why I was so chuffed to have my *Little Book of Lists* notebook out earlier this year – when I held the first official copy of it straight from the printers, it took me right back to the day I got my school planner.

One day I'd love to have a full stationery range; that would be a dream come true. Zoflora-scented gel pens are the future, surely! Can you imagine?

I might have had the most organised and colour coordinated planner in the whole of Year 7, but I'm not academically smart by any stretch and I struggled with the core subjects of English, Maths and Science. They just didn't come naturally and it used to panic me that I wasn't much good at them because it had always been drummed into us how important they were if we wanted to have a successful future. So then I'd put extra pressure on myself, get into a right mess and end up doing worse.

Turns out, I've never really needed them. I've got a calculator for sums and I definitely don't need to know how a rock erodes. What I *did* need to know but was never taught were life skills, things like how tax works, paying bills, insurance, pensions, saving, cleaning, organising and how to change a tyre.

I think it would be great if schools could focus a bit more on these sorts of things so that kids leave school better equipped for the real world.

Weirdly, though, I loved French. I'm not too sure why, but it might have been to do with the fact that everyone started at the same level and so I felt really equal in that class. I also loved learning something new.

Me and Jamie have said we'd really like to learn a second language so we're thinking about starting an evening class together. Jamie is already quite clued up with Spanish because his parents lived in Spain for so long, and it's something we could do together.

My French teacher was actually French herself and very sophisticated. She was really tall with beautiful black curly hair and bright red lipstick, and I thought: 'Wow, she's amazing.'

She'd say '*bonjour*' to everyone as we walked into class and I thought that was so cool! So I really enjoyed those lessons.

I also liked cookery, funnily enough. I know I'm no Nigella in the kitchen, but I enjoy trying and I really liked creating things, and obviously the tidying away massively appealed. Old habits clearly die hard . . .

PE, though, used to give me pure anxiety because I hated getting undressed in the changing rooms. Going through puberty where everyone is developing at different speeds is a really difficult time, especially for girls. Some would be there in their proper bras whereas my mum would make me wear babyish cropped tops, just to cover my little nips, and I'd feel really embarrassed of that.

It was around this time I became very aware of my body and my height in particular, as I seemed to be growing far quicker than everyone else. I started to feel very self-conscious and I'm going to talk more about how negative body image has affected me throughout my life later on in this book.

This lack of confidence was made worse by the fact that the group of girls I was supposed to be friends with started to exclude me in a pretty harsh way.

It's something I touched on in *Hinch Yourself Happy*, and while it wasn't ever physical bullying, it was emotional and mental torture and meant I lived with a constant worry.

Every morning I'd go into school on tenterhooks, feeling sick not knowing if I was going to be included that day or not. Were they going to be my friends or was I going to have to spend the day on my own?

If one of them smiled at me when I walked into the classroom, the relief that washed over me was immense. It was a sign that OK, today is going to be fine.

But a lot of the time I got the silent treatment. They'd deliberately walk off at a quicker pace in front of me, whispering to each other. I'd be left behind trying to keep up with them, feeling embarrassed but pretending not to notice that they were trying to get away from me. I'd be running along after them and attempting to join in with whatever they were laughing at.

Knowing I had to go to school made me feel trapped. I'd be up through the night on the toilet with a nervous tummy, terrified of what lay ahead the next day, and I actually ended up losing quite a bit of weight during that time.

I'd dread certain days, depending on what lessons we had. For instance, I knew on a Thursday there were three lessons which they'd all be in and that meant there was a big chance they'd have decided to leave me out. I hated Thursdays.

It was never-ending mind games, and they were always pushing me away – I often felt very lonely.

This went on for the best part of Year 7, which feels like a lifetime when you're twelve.

I'd say it's definitely affected me going into adulthood and means I worry about Ronnie ever suffering in the same way. I actually get really emotional about Ronnie going to school. What if he has no friends? What if he gets pushed over in his little uniform? I couldn't bear it!

I also think it's one of the reasons I like to use my platform to help anyone who's a bit of an outsider or who is on their own and struggling. I've always had this burning need to help people in some way – I just never thought it would be like this.

I've thought long and hard about why it was me who was left out. Why was I their target? I know I was a very needy child (I still am!) and, in their defence, I must have been annoying.

I know you should never blame the victim in cases of bullying, but I do wonder whether in trying to be liked by too many people, I got on everyone's nerves. I get that. I constantly needed reassurance that they were OK with me and still liked me, so maybe I was a bit of a paranoid irritant.

My mum went to speak to one of their mums once and asked if they could please get all of us together and do something. But that made it worse, if I'm honest. They ended up using that against me – it just gave them another reason to hate me and leave me out.

Shortly after *Hinch Yourself Happy* was published, where I'd shared a bit about my experience, I received a message from one of the girls. She had never been the ringleader but she was part of the group, and I could have thrown up when I saw her name pop up in my DMs.

All those feelings of worry came flooding back.

But it was actually the most amazing message and gave me a chance, I suppose, to put to bed what was a very hard time in my life. She said she'd read the book, knew exactly who I was referring to and that she was really sorry that she'd ever made me feel that way. She said she'd had a lot going on in her life when we were in Year 7 and she was much happier now.

I replied and said thank you for getting in touch and told her that I didn't hold any grudges. Because I don't; we were young, all trying to make our way through life, and I genuinely do wish them all the best.

I think 'closure' would be too strong a word to use, but her message did give me something to think about. Clearly she had a lot on her plate at the time it was all going on and she wasn't a completely happy child herself.

The only time I experienced anything physical at school was a one-off incident at the vending machine where I'd just bought a chocolate bar. I was in Year 7 and this boy who was in the year above demanded that I hand it over to him.

'No,' I said. 'I've just paid for it!'

He had a plaster cast on his arm and, no word of a lie, he whacked me over the head with it continuously until I finally screamed at him to just take the bloody chocolate bar. My head hurt.

No one else was around so he got away with it, but when I went home and told my sister, she went mad. Sam is very feisty – me and her are complete opposites – and she asked me who had done it.

I knew who it was – I even know his full name to this day – but I said I didn't because she would 100 per cent have stormed up to the school the next day and stood over him while he bought me a new chocolate bar. She takes absolutely no shit! I figured it was best to keep quiet because I certainly didn't need anything else to make things even harder than they already were.

During secondary school, Mum and Dad let me have a pet rabbit who I named Barney. I was lucky to have him because he got me through so many of the hard times. I thought the world of him. I stayed in my room, broken-hearted, for days after he passed away. Poor Barney. I even kept the rich tea biscuit he'd been nibbling on, on the way to the vet's to be put to sleep. His last meal! I've still got it in a memory box in my mum and dad's loft, totally intact, no sign of mould. That's lasted the best part of twenty years, so it makes you wonder what on earth those biscuits are made of!

Everything changed for the better the day I met Tanya for the first time. As normal, I was Billy No-Mates, sitting on the stairs on my own eating my lunch, when she came up to me and asked me what on earth I was doing down there.

We already knew each other a bit from primary and started chatting. She invited me round to her house after school. I accepted, and soon after that we joined up with the rest of the girls, and the five of us – the kids, as we call each other – have been inseparable ever since.

We weren't the popular girls, although we weren't unpopular either. We were just the in-betweeners, if you like.

We've stuck together through everything, which is pretty mad, and I couldn't ever be without them. They know I'm needy but have always accepted me just as I am. They'd joke that I needed to go with the flow a bit more but were never horrible about it, and I've always felt able to be my true self around them. I'm so grateful that I have them in my life.

As we got older, we started to notice boys a bit more, and I was thirteen when I had my first kiss. He was a local boy who lived round the close.

My mum and his mum were friends, so we'd known each other since we were toddlers, and I remember he used to have a Thomas the Tank Engine kite which we'd go and fly. Isn't it funny the little details you remember like that?

He was such a popular, sociable kid and when my dad used to wash the car he'd come up to our house and happily chat away. He was the one who would knock on your door and always be first out to play.

Anyway, we were walking back from what was Safeway at the time (that's a blast from the past, isn't it?) and out of the blue he stopped and kissed me. It took me by surprise, but it was a very welcome one!

He was tall and broad with the biggest brown eyes and thick silky hair. I remember him being so handsome.

He became my first boyfriend after that. One of my friends ended up going out with his best mate and the four of us used to go round in a little group.

It fizzled out after a few months as most teen romances do, but neither of us were heartbroken and we stayed friends. We lost touch with each other as we got older and moved away, although my mum would keep me updated on his news and I always loved to hear about him.

It was in February 2018 I got a phone call from one of

the kids that left me really shaken. She called to say that he had taken his own life.

I couldn't speak. I still get upset talking about it now and I know it really hit my mum hard because she was close to his family and had watched him grow up. I'd not seen him for several years, but I have the fondest memories of him and he was so loved.

I couldn't believe that someone who had such a safe haven at home, with lovely brothers and amazing parents, someone who was funny, healthy and, by all accounts, had everything to live for, had done something like that. He was always the funny one, the one who made everyone laugh, so it just didn't make any sense. I don't know the ins and outs of what led him to do what he did. I feel so sad for him that he felt so troubled.

They do a memorial walk every year around the town for him and he's buried in the same cemetery as the dad of one of my friends. It's a beautiful place. Me and the girls sometimes go up there, as she was the first one of us to lose a parent and we all loved her dad so much. We go to the McDonald's drive-thru first and take a picnic there and I always take time to walk past his grave, to pay my respects and remember him.

I still can't quite get my head round it. It's such a harsh world.

Thankfully, I've not lost a family member or close friend as of yet. My mum's mum is still alive but both my grandads and my dad's mum passed away before I was born. I wish I'd got to meet them, to hear their voices. And I'd love to have seen my mum with her dad.

I know I'm so lucky not to have experienced true loss or grief yet, but I know it will happen because death is part of life and that scares me. I wake up and worry about it and wonder who is going to be taken from me.

Although I had adored my first boyfriend, it was only a very innocent relationship and I was never really interested in dating. Walking round holding hands with a boy just never appealed to me. To be honest, I've shed more tears over girls than I ever have over boys.

I was always there for my kids when they were broken-hearted, but I guess having a boyfriend myself would have only been something else to add to the endless list of things to worry about.

I did sometimes feel left out, though, and I just got this feeling that I got on the boys' nerves when we went out in a mixed group or I played the third wheel.

I know a lot of my friends' boyfriends were wary of me because I was very protective of my kids and so if their fellas weren't being nice to them or they'd kissed another girl, I'd tell them. Damn right I would!

Sometimes that would mean the girls would get annoyed with me too, although they do thank me for it now. I'll say no more than that, but they'll be reading this and will know exactly what I'm talking about! It was only ever because I love them so much.

Going out with boys and heading off to parties and

hanging around in the park simply wasn't my idea of fun. I just wanted to be at home with my mum and dad having a Chinese takeaway and watching the TV. I used to highlight the programmes I wanted to watch in the TV guide and that's what made me feel happy and safe. It's funny how some things don't change.

I'd be planning what I was going to watch on the telly that night while the others were planning what heels they were going to wear to go out in.

I tried it now and again, going out to a few little parties here and there, but I never enjoyed it. I'd stay for a couple of hours before going home and I wasn't allowed out too late anyway.

I mostly only ever drank to appease others, and whenever I did try WKD, Lambrini or White Lightning (we've all done it!) the results were horrendous. I didn't like the feeling of being drunk or even tipsy and going home and trying to hide it from my mum and dad. And then waking up the next morning and feeling embarrassed and worried about what I'd said or done was just the worst.

I experimented with alcohol as all youngsters do, but I was never going to be a big drinker and I didn't give my parents much to worry about during my teens. My mum would say that too. I was a good kid.

I left school after my GCSEs and went to sixth form college to do A-levels, but I left before I completed them. It's sad, but I never felt like that next step was achievable for me. I used to struggle to remember things – my memory is like a sieve – so I go to pieces in exams and I used to get so frustrated and upset with myself.

I always wanted to be a primary school teacher and if I could go back and do it all again, I think I'd give that my best shot. I've always had an eye for kids who aren't enjoying their life as much as they should be and wanted to help them.

I also fancied becoming a midwife and with everything that's happened this year, it made me wish I'd pushed myself with that. But I dismissed it out of hand before I could even really think about it.

Like with a lot of things, I discounted it assuming I would never get there. Now, I reckon if I'd had a bit more faith in myself and put my mind to it, I could have done it. If I'd tried, I could have done something really meaningful, although weirdly I've ended up helping more people than I could have ever imagined in a way I didn't think was possible.

The truth was, I wasn't too sure about where I wanted to go in life or what I wanted to do, and what had once appeared to be a mere tendency to worry was now often crippling me.

I know my mum and dad were upset at the thought of me being held back by myself and of my being unhappy because I was on edge all the time.

They were mostly worried about how extremely sensitive I was and the insecurities and anxiety that seemed to be gripping me tighter and tighter the older I got.

And I had no idea how to get it under control.

# Three

# Anxiety

I've always been a worrier, for as long as I can remember. I'm naturally an over-thinker and lose ridiculous amounts of sleep fretting over pretty much anything and everything.

You name it, I'll find the stress in it! It's quite a skill actually.

I know a lot of you can relate to what I'm describing here. I get so many DMs from my followers who feel the same and it really helps me to realise that none of us are alone. Before I got to know you lot, I felt a bit like the odd one out and had no idea that having these worries was so common.

We really are in this together and I hope you never forget that.

I'm no good at being the centre of attention. I'm not comfortable in the spotlight and I make myself ill worrying about what people think of me. I really am trying my best to work on that, though. When things are going well, I automatically think: 'I don't deserve this, my life is too good, surely something bad must be around the corner.'

I can't shake off the feeling that whatever I have is too great to be true and so I'm always just waiting for something to go wrong. Whenever I start to let myself feel happy, that's when my anxiety kicks in. It has the effect of swallowing me up and it means any happiness I feel is only ever for a short time and I feel like I'm never able to fully live in the moment and just enjoy it.

Gosh, actually writing that down makes me feel a bit sad. Like I'm finally acknowledging it out loud. I so often wish I wasn't like this.

Worrying far too much is part of who I am. Right from when I was a little baby my mum tells me I was very clingy and needy towards her. I still am, if I'm honest! Even if I was somewhere as familiar as my nan's house, when Mum left the room to go to the loo, I'd not feel settled and look for her until she came back.

I think she tried every nursery this side of Chelmsford before she found somewhere I felt comfortable in. I just didn't want to be away from her and that's the reason I ended up going to nursery quite a bit later than other children my age.

She eventually found one where there was a lovely, warm lady I felt an instant bond with – Mrs Woss was her name. Finding someone I connected with was always – and still is – the key to me feeling calmer and more relaxed in any situation. Even so, I never lost the dependence on my mum.

When I started going to primary school, I would come home every lunchtime rather than stay and eat in the dinner hall with all the other kids. Mum would come and collect me each day and I'd have a jacket potato with cheese in the lounge while we watched *101 Dalmatians*.

Just knowing she was coming to pick me up at midday helped me get through the morning. It gave me something to focus on and look forward to. I'm sure having to travel back and forth more than she needed to every day must have been so annoying for my poor mum! Now I'm a mummy myself I understand that you do everything in your power to keep your babies happy, but she definitely went above and beyond.

She'd drop me back at school at 1 p.m. and I knew I only had a couple more hours before I saw her again. So that was OK and I was able to make it through the afternoon quite happily.

I had loads of friends at primary school, so everything was fine from that perspective, but I needed a lot of reassurance in the classroom and I would be constantly checking with the teacher that what I was doing was right. I remember Mrs Wright in Year 6 saying: 'Sophie Barker, you're at my desk more than you are your own!'

She was probably right, to be fair.

A lot of the worrying I did came from lacking self-confidence and genuinely being bothered by what other people thought of me. I was a people pleaser and just wanted to be liked but also never felt worthy enough.

In Year 3 I remember convincing myself that the teacher Mrs Dolphin didn't like me. I haven't got a clue what it was that made me think that – probably something and nothing, knowing me – but it was eating me up and making me not want to go into school full stop.

My mum and dad had to go and see the headteacher to try and sort things out and they asked about whether or not I'd be able to switch classes. In the end, that's what happened and I moved to Mrs Brown's class . . . but then I was worried that Mrs Dolphin would hate me even more for asking to move.

I adored Mrs Brown, though, and I was a lot happier going to school after that.

As I got older, the feelings of anxiousness got much more intense.

Naturally, as you grow up in life and you have more responsibilities, you tend to have more and more things to worry about, and every time I left the house I'd stress about even the littlest of things, like getting to places on time, which bus stop to leave from and who was picking me up. Things anyone else wouldn't have given more than a couple of seconds' thought would flood my head until it didn't seem worth the hassle of going out at all.

My friends would all be excited to be meeting up and as

much as I wanted to join in, I could never get my mind off how I was getting there and back and how long I'd be away from home. It would use up all my energy, and looking back, it really limited how much of a social life I had as a young girl.

I wouldn't – couldn't – ever go to sleepovers. I didn't even like playing at other people's houses after school. I was fine if they could come to me but I didn't want to be away from my mum.

Even after I put what happened at secondary school behind me and met the kids and had that tight support network around me, it still wasn't something I seemed to be able to get over.

I'd turn down invitations to parties, I'd constantly worry about being talked about behind my back, I'd stew over what so-and-so really thought of me and only ever felt completely safe when I was at home.

Even now most of what I get worked up over are things I can't control, which I realise is completely pointless, but they constantly niggle away at me anyway. And over the years, that worrying has moved on and turned into full-blown anxiety and it's something I'm constantly battling with.

I try to keep it away from my Instagram because it's not what my account is about, but you guys can always tell when I'm having an off day and I really do appreciate it so much when you get in touch to check on me.

After dropping out of sixth form I had a few jobs, one of which was working for a recruitment agency in

Chelmsford. I met some new friends there but even then I'd call my mum and ask her to drive over from Maldon and meet me for lunch.

When I remember that now, it seems so mad. I mean, how embarrassing being a fully grown adult in a professional job and ringing your mum to ask her to meet you for lunch! But sometimes it felt like the only way I could get through the day.

So, every lunchtime my colleagues would go to places like the nearby noodle bar or a nice deli and I'd call my mum who would drive the twenty-minute journey from Maldon for us to sit on the bench in the churchyard and eat our sandwiches.

I loved that time together but then I'd spend the last ten minutes of my break panicking about having to go back to the office again. What a nightmare it all was.

It wasn't like the people there left me out or ignored me. They were lovely. It was more the case that they were confident enough to do their own thing at lunch and I felt quite lost. They all seemed really cool and good at their jobs, going out to meet clients, and I just felt so different to them.

I didn't look like them, for a start.

I had been gaining a lot of weight and was becoming very aware of my size and that made me feel like I just didn't fit in. I wanted so badly to be able to wear a little suit and heels like the rest of the girls who always looked so smart and glam, but I didn't feel like those things would look right on me. I was so overweight that I struggled to find a pair of tailored trousers and a blazer that fitted nicely around my bust.

Instead, I ended up wearing these elasticated waist pants and jackets that didn't match because they were the nearest thing to a 'suit' I could find to fit me.

All of these insecurities built up in my head and by the end of my time there, I had pure dread going in every day. And annoyingly, I was actually quite good at the job and enjoyed speaking to people on the phone, but it was hopeless. I was getting more and more anxious about the whole thing and something had to change.

I only stayed for nine months before handing in my notice and moving to Witham to work at an apprenticeship college.

My job there was to find placements for apprentices and it turned out to be a life changer because it was where I met one of my now-best friends, Trace. We hit it off straightaway.

On my first day, the managing director came in and said: 'Girls, I'm going to Morrisons to get some lunch. Is there anything you'd like?'

And I said: 'Ooh, yes, please, I'll have a wrap. Just as long as it's not a duck wrap!'

I'm not a fan of a duck wrap.

So, off she went to Morrisons and when she came back she said: 'Hello, dear, I've got you a duck wrap.'

Well. Me and Trace were sat there and I could see her

shoulders shaking from trying not to laugh. I said thank you for the wrap, handed her the money and then sat at my desk trying to eat it because I didn't want to be rude.

I was almost gagging because I really hate duck wraps and all that hoisin sauce!

I'd never really spoken to Trace at this point but after a few seconds she leaned over and said, trying to keep a straight face: 'How's your wrap?'

And that was it. We just burst out laughing. Like, uncontrollably crying with laughter until it actually hurt our stomachs. I'd not belly-laughed like that in a long time.

Once we'd composed ourselves Trace said she was going to Morrisons herself and asked if she could get me something else instead. I gratefully accepted her offer and she gave me her number so I could text her what I wanted on the quiet.

She actually messaged me later that night to say she was still cracking up laughing at me sitting trying to eat this bloody duck wrap (I was too! I still giggle now just thinking about it) and from that day, we've been stuck together like glue. We laughed and laughed every day. We've been laughing ever since, if I'm honest.

Trace is only a year older than me and we were so similar in so many ways. Neither of us was great at make-up although we gave it our best shot; we both loved our food; we both suffered with our nerves and we also both wore an old black cardigan every single day because it was the only thing we felt good in.

We became the best of friends, and we still call each other 'duck wrap' now and no one else knows what on earth we're talking about! I guess they will now, right?

I loved the job itself, too, so it was a win-win. A lot of it involved working alongside older lecturers and I was actually more comfortable with them than I had been with the young and trendy sales consultants over in Chelmsford!

I didn't feel any competition or have people to compare myself to, which felt like such a relief. It was me and Trace and we basically found ourselves in a room together with a load of forty-plus tutors, and they became our friends.

When she eventually left to go and set up her nail business, I struggled to be there without her. I guess that's what I mean about always wanting someone around me who I love and trust so that I feel relaxed.

The company was slowly closing down anyway and so I decided to leave too and got myself a job in London working at a recruitment company. Which is where I met Jamie, funnily enough, so it turned out to be the best decision I ever made!

It was a big step for me. But I would never have even considered moving to London on my own, so I commuted in each day from Essex. I'm not sure if it was the pressure of starting a new job or being in a city that was strange to me, but I suffered the first panic attack of my life shortly after I started working there.

There was nothing specific that triggered it – it just happened without any warning and it was terrifying – but maybe it was inevitable after all those years of worrying. In a way I'm surprised I reached my early twenties before I had one.

I was in the toilets at work and felt this weird sensation creeping up my back and then tightening in my chest. I was finding it difficult to breathe and I didn't know what it was. I remember thinking: 'Why is this not going away?'

It felt like my heart was beating out of my chest which started me panicking even more, and the more I panicked the worse it got. It was thumping so hard it felt like I was being punched from the inside.

I was supposed to go into a training session, so in my mind I had no choice but to stumble out of the Ladies and make my way to the boardroom. I had to get there because the thought of being late and having everyone turn and look at me was making me even worse. And I didn't want my boss to tell me off!

I somehow managed to get to the training even though I was still tingling and all het up, and I felt like the whole room knew what had happened as I sat there with my chest pounding, sweating all over and my face bright red.

I think it was only afterwards that I put two and two together and realised what had happened to me and that it had been a full-blown panic attack.

Weirdly, I didn't have another one for quite a while after that. I'd met Jamie, and although we were just friends at that point, he's always had a very calming effect on me and we had a great connection right from the off. I started to become more settled and secure and working there made me feel like I was part of something.

The attacks really only began again once Mrs Hinch took off and I started getting attention on a level I never expected and would have normally gone out of my way to avoid.

In *Hinch Yourself Happy* I wrote about a particularly bad one on the plane on the way back from our honeymoon which came out of nowhere. There doesn't have to be a trigger – sometimes they can come on and I'm completely blindsided. I'm always helpless to them.

They can also take slightly different forms. In February this year when I turned thirty, I had such a weird attack of I don't know what. It wasn't a panic attack as such, not like what I've been used to in the past. I'd say it was more of an anxiety overload.

I honestly wasn't bothered about getting older – age is irrelevant to me and so the number thirty didn't mean anything. It was more to do with the milestone of leaving my twenties behind when so much in my life had changed in that decade. It was the evening of my birthday and I was on holiday in Disneyland, lying on the hotel bed, and I found myself crying so much that I couldn't catch my breath.

I was scared to enter my thirties because I don't know what they're going to bring. I'm excited but frightened. I don't feel in control. I miss my twenties so much because of the completely normal life I had then. My thirties feel like they're going to be a very different experience.

I hope that makes sense.

My anxiety was probably as bad as it has ever been at the start of this year. After trying to brush it under the carpet for several years, I found myself in a really dark place and I knew something had shifted. In the past I had been drifting along but was still able to manage it, whereas now I was very definitely falling. I was physically and emotionally exhausted and felt like I had nothing left to give.

I'm absolutely terrible when it comes to asking for help and I kept putting off going to the doctor because I was worried they'd look at me and think: 'What on earth has she got to be depressed or anxious about?'

And I know that on the surface, I do have a very lovely life. But mental health doesn't discriminate – it can affect anyone – and behind the scenes I was falling apart.

I was getting hot flushes, was struggling to get to sleep and constantly had that feeling in my tummy you get when you haven't eaten and it aches. I had chronic diarrhoea because my stomach was working overtime. Whenever I ate anything, I'd be straight on the toilet. Sorry, TMI!

I was waking up all through the night in a sweat and spending hours feeling just wired, worrying, thinking, struggling to breathe and beating myself up for something I'd done that day, or hadn't done or should have done differently.

Even something as small as the way I said goodbye to someone I'd stopped to chat to on the street would play on my mind.

And then all that sleeplessness would mean I was running on empty the next day. Each morning it was harder to get out of bed and I could feel myself sinking further and further. I stopped leaving the house because the world felt petrifying to me and I didn't feel like I could go out. I was struggling to see the light.

Eventually, much to the relief of my family who I know were worried sick about me, I booked an appointment with my GP who recommended I start on antidepressants.

I've never been on that kind of medication before and so I was extremely wary of taking it. But I was also desperate to feel better and it felt like I had run out of other options. My mum convinced me that there was no shame in having a little tablet, not to change who I am but just to level things out a bit.

It took a few weeks to feel the effects of the medication I was given, but what it's done has made me a bit numb, which I guess is a good thing. Things don't feel as heightened as they used to and it's taken a bit of the bite away. At least I've stopped getting worse, but now I'm scared to ever come off them in case I fall again.

It's interesting how people look at mental health, isn't

it? If there was something wrong with my arm or my leg, I wouldn't think anything at all of going to the doctor and getting whatever treatment I needed to fix that. But we don't see our heads in the same way. I think we need to do more of that.

I'm doing OK on the tablets. They made me feel travel sick at first but that only lasted for a few days and so the side effects haven't been too bad. I'm still worrying every day, but I feel like the edge has been taken off and so I can power through regardless. I'm finding it a lot easier to get up and start the day and crack on.

I still have that knot in my tummy, though. I get it especially bad in the evenings, worrying about what the night will bring and whether I'm going to be able to sleep.

I've accepted that no matter what I do in life, whether I'm in front of one person or 3 million, I'm probably always going to have these feelings.

One of the things I'm constantly fighting is the fear of letting people down. Every Hincher I meet, I walk away afterwards feeling anxious that they're disappointed in me. I get scared that they might think I'm not as 'good' as they thought I would be and then I spend ages replaying and thinking about what I said, how I was with them, what I looked like. Could I have said something different? Did I give them enough of my time? Did I help them?

Thinking, thinking. Overthinking.

I know that's not a healthy state of mind to be in but I don't know how to turn it off.

This is the first time I've ever really spoken about this in detail and it's quite hard for me to open up about it. I suppose it's tough admitting out loud that something is 'wrong' when I've always wanted to present an image of a woman who is in control and living her best life.

My platform is known for being positive and picking people up and making them laugh, and I don't feel like I ever want to show myself getting upset or admit that I'm struggling. If I can make people smile just once a day then that makes me happy, so even when I'm having a really bad day you will still see me being a bit silly and having fun on my stories. And actually, I find the distraction really helps.

Doing that has been harder than ever this year, to be honest with you. It was a real challenge finding the right balance during the Coronavirus pandemic, which I really believe has changed our world forever.

I tried to keep my content cheerful so people had somewhere to come to escape, to forget about the sadness and the fear we were all experiencing, but at the same time I couldn't ignore it. It's one of the biggest events we'll live through and it was affecting everyone's lives in the most extreme and frightening ways and I had to acknowledge that, on a human level at least.

I know for many of you, my Instagram helps you to switch off from the outside world, even if it's just for a little while, but it wouldn't have been right to not at least recognise what was going on. So I tried to keep things as normal as possible.

You'd message me to say thank you for making you laugh even for a few seconds. I couldn't reply to everyone but I shared some of the DMs so people knew they weren't alone.

It was so hard to get that right. I really hope I managed it.

People were anxious and understandably so. It got so serious so quickly, didn't it? It went from something that was happening in China to all of a sudden none of us being able to live our normal lives and see our families, which was heart-breaking.

I missed my family so much. But I couldn't moan. People were dying alone without their loved ones being able to comfort them in their final moments and I just couldn't get my head around that. It's just so awful.

I constantly reminded myself that I was lucky to love my home and feel safe there. I looked on it not as being trapped but as being safe. Nothing can replace a cuddle, but we have so many ways of connecting with each other these days and we made use of apps like Zoom and Face-Time to stay in touch.

It made me realise how fragile and unpredictable life is. There was this silent, invisible killer that none of us saw coming and there was absolutely nothing we could do about it.

I am convinced there will be positives to come from what we've all been through. It's brought communities closer together because people looked out for and got to know their neighbours. We rediscovered the joys of the simple things in life and I don't think we'll ever take them for granted again.

It made us appreciate our incredible NHS more than ever before, didn't it? Jamie and I did the Clap for Carers every Thursday evening and hearing everyone else around us doing the same was so moving. A lot of my Hinchers work in the NHS and you all told me how much it meant to you to hear that applause.

All the key workers were heroes. The people doing deliveries and those working on the shop floors were keeping the country running and the shelves stocked up. They are amongst the most underpaid and under-acknowledged, but when it came to a global crisis, they were the people we absolutely needed.

My mum actually said at the time: 'There's something behind all of this, Soph. Something amazing.'

So maybe after all this terrible hardship and tragedy, we'll start treating the world and each other with more love and respect. Hopefully we'll look back on this year as the wake-up call we needed to sort ourselves out.

Time will tell.

Obviously it affected me mentally, although weirdly, not specifically my anxiety like you might expect. My emotions were just all over the place. I feel like a lot of people's were. It was like being on this non-stop roller-coaster of moods.

I'd wake up in the morning and forget for a split second and then remember that I wanted to make sure everyone was OK. So there was a lot of worry and stress, but I didn't come close to a panic attack over it and I think a lot of that was down to the support and love I felt from my Hinchers telling me we were going to get through it together.

I also used my usual coping mechanisms to distract myself. I really enjoy doing the random activities in my *Activity Journal*. Yes, I'm thirty years old and I'm a proud dot-to-dotter! Some people might think it's childish, but we've all got to do what it takes to get us through the day and dot-to-dots really help me switch off. So does writing out my Hinch Lists and reading my positive affirmations every day. I post one each night on my stories before bed and maybe by sharing them, other people can feel better too.

I hope so.

Caring about so many people can sometimes feel like a big responsibility. I love having you all there, but I worry that people need me and I can't always reach them.

Sometimes followers message me and say they're really struggling and that they don't want to be here any more.

Just the other day a woman got in touch saying: 'I don't want to wake up tomorrow. Can you help me?'

I could never ignore a message like that – if anything

ever happened, I couldn't live with myself. Like what if I didn't see that message? How many messages like that haven't I seen? It worries me so much.

What people are going through on their own is often so upsetting. They have no one, so they talk to me. And I'm so happy that I can be there and people feel comfortable opening up to me. My DMs are always open. I often lie awake at night thinking and thinking about those people and worrying about them, wondering how they are. I feel personally responsible.

The We Love Mrs Hinch group on Facebook is such a lovely community where people support each other all day long. I scroll through the posts a lot and you guys on there have no idea how much you give me; just seeing all this love on a group set up in my name is incredible. If I ever see a post that worries me, I try to reach out privately to those people I think might need a bit more support.

Earlier this year I decided to try and take one day off a week where I had a 24-hour social media shut down. As much as I try to stick to it, I haven't always managed it, mainly because part of me thinks it's taking the piss. Like, I don't deserve a day off because people would prefer me to be 'on'.

There are people waiting for me to post my next story, to shine my sink, put the cloths away, chop the cushions and say goodnight, and I don't ever want to let anyone down.

I'm still trying to figure that out and feel very undecided about what the right thing to do is. When I've managed to take a full day off, I come back feeling refreshed and ready to take everything on again, so it's definitely worth it from a personal point of view.

I sometimes feel pulled and stretched in different directions and I'm scared that one day I'm going to snap. And on the days I struggle the most, if I could turn back the clock to my life before, I would do it in a heartbeat. To not be Mrs Hinch just for a while . . . and then I even feel bad for feeling like that, because I don't want to ever seem like I'm not grateful. Because I really, really am, but life was just a lot simpler then.

I'll come to the trolls later in this book and the impact they've had on my family and my own mental health, but even a post as joyful as my pregnancy reveal picture on Christmas Day in 2018 wasn't off limits.

What sort of person sees a pregnancy announcement as an opportunity to be nasty?

Jamie is a fantastic support, but at the same time he doesn't have anxiety or panic attacks, so I don't think he'll ever fully understand.

The only one who really calms me down is Henry. Maybe it's because he can't talk, which means he can't say anything wrong!

Hinching is still my number one way to beat my anxiety. It might only be cleaning out the toaster but if I've achieved that, I feel more at ease. I found myself cleaning twice as much as I normally do during the lockdown – you might have noticed on my stories! I don't think my house has ever been so shiny!

It was when I went back to college to study hairdressing in the evenings a few years ago, when my mum popped round to the flat Jamie and I were renting and brought with her a bottle of Zoflora – Bouquet was the scent – and from there on I discovered just how much cleaning calmed me down.

I loved finding new products and building up my collection of favourites in what would later become my Narnia. It became more than just a hobby to me – I couldn't get enough!

Before and after pictures are a big thing for me – I like to take a picture of the mess, get going on it and then take a picture when it's done, and seeing that helps my mind settle and makes me feel proud. I call them my achievement pictures.

And the ticks are also part of that. Even one little tick a day on my Hinch List is enough and I'm happy. I never feel the need to rush them because I know they will get done and the ticks are a real visual sign of how far I've got.

Talking about how I feel helps me too. Admitting it. I feel like a weight has been lifted just by sharing it all with you here. And I really hope by writing about it, I can help other people feeling like this.

I don't know all the answers but I'm getting better at

accepting that it's OK not to. When I was younger, I honestly thought I'd have it all figured out by this age and I don't at all! Not even close.

But really, how boring would life be if we all had it figured out by thirty or forty or even fifty?

I'm learning to love the fact that I've still got loads of stuff to find out about the world, other people and myself.

That is life. It's confusing and scary at times but we've all got to try and find a way of muddling through it as best we can. We could all be kinder to ourselves, I think.

Of course, it's always easier to do that when you've got people by your side who understand you and love you. Which I definitely do.

I have amazing friends and family, and I have you guys too. All of that gives me such a lot of strength and makes the tougher times much easier to manage.

## A Bit More About Me

A few things you may not have known about me . . .

### My perfect day . . .

Getting dressed, popping out to B&M for a Hinch Haul, coming home and pottering about in the garden. Then dinner, sofa and *EastEnders* with my handsomes.

## My worst habit . . .

Making a mountain out of a molehill.

## Being in love feels like . . .

It makes you feel full, whole and no longer missing a piece.

## My dream dinner party guests . . .

All three grandparents who I sadly never got to meet. I'd love to hear stories about my parents from when they were younger and what they got up to.

## My greatest strength . . .

I keep going even when I'm about to drop. I don't give up easily.

## My celebrity crush . . .

Danny Dyer. I do like a geezer. His daughter Dani from *Love Island* messaged me and she was so nice but I was also thinking: 'I actually quite fancy your dad!'

## My guiltiest pleasure . . .

Watching *Bargain Hunt*. I love going to car boot sales and finding little treasures.

### I get angry at . . .

The lies about me on the internet.

### My favourite film . . .

I love *Taken*, *The Borrowers* and *The Pursuit of Happyness*. But I'll also never get bored of watching *Mary Poppins*!

### The possession I'd rescue
### from a burning building . . .

Ronnie's baby book. It's so precious to me.

### My superpower would be . . .

To freeze time. Everything is flying by so fast. Ronnie is growing up so quickly and I just want our lives to stay together like this forever.

### My last meal would be . . .

My mum's roast chicken dinner.

### My party trick is . . .

I'm not bad at beatboxing. Oh, and I can do a Mexican wave with my tongue. I'll have to put it on my stories one day!

### My proudest moment . . .

Seeing Jamie holding Ronnie for the first time.

### My most embarrassing moment . . .

Getting Durex and Dulux mixed up on my stories. Not only did millions of people see it at the time, but it ended up in the papers. Mortified. An easy mistake to make . . .

### My biggest regret . . .

I try not to have them. I think it's better to learn from everything and move on.

### My spirit animal is . . .

A penguin. They find their mate and they're with them for life and I love that.

### Coffee or tea?

Tea. Every time.

### My favourite biscuit . . .

Oreos. Or a good old traditional Malted Milk.

**The song played at my funeral would be . . .**

'I Was Here', Beyoncé.

**My epitaph . . .**

All the best!

# Four

## Jamie

On paper, me and Jamie are like chalk and cheese. He's an easy-going, no stress, water-off-a-duck's-back kind of guy and takes everything in his stride.

Me? Er, not so much! I wish I was more like that. But you know what they say about opposites . . . and in a strange way, it just works. We work.

Although he might look like this big, hard man, that couldn't be further from the truth. He's actually really soft and gentle. He's very emotional and isn't ever afraid to show his feelings. And he's even cheesier than I am! If you can believe it.

Not many people know this, but he's actually eleven years older than me, although I forget his age, if I'm honest.

We only ever really notice the age gap when we're talking about things like music and I'll call the stuff he loves from the 80s and 90s the tunes from his 'era'! He quite often suggests the tracks I put on my stories when I Hinch.

But it's obvious we come from very different worlds – in fact, I often say he's from the 'real world'.

Jamie was born in Enfield and grew up in Southgate, North London, where life was tough and he had to learn to be streetwise and savvy from a very young age. I've lived a very sheltered life compared to him, growing up in the middle of nowhere, where people would happily leave their front doors unlocked, kids played out in the street all day long and everyone knew their neighbours.

I'll never forget the first time he came to visit me at my parents' house in Maldon in the summer of 2013, not long after we'd started going out. I left my bike out the front of the house and he was absolutely horrified.

'You can't leave that there!' he said.

'Yeah, it's fine,' I replied.

'But . . . but . . . you need to lock it away!'

'Nah, it'll be OK there overnight. I'm using it again in the morning.'

He looked at me in complete and utter shock. He honestly thought I was joking because he comes from a place where you bolt everything up or nail it down or else it gets nicked.

He couldn't believe how relaxed and safe everything was, and coming to deepest Essex felt like paradise to him with all the freedom, fresh air and green fields. We still only live a mile away from where I grew up, but we both appreciate it every day and I know we always will.

While our upbringings might have been very different, what we do share are the things I think are the most important. We have the same morals, beliefs and principles, and family is front and centre of everything for both of us.

Me and my family live in each other's pockets. We're all just a few minutes down the road from one another and I couldn't ever have it any other way. Family is my life. Jamie's family are more spread out but they have so much love for each other. It's amazing. We make sure that we get together with them as much as possible.

Both sets of our parents are still together, which is so rare these days – mine have been married for over twenty-six years and Jamie's for more than forty. How's that for marriage goals? Simply incredible.

I was twenty-two when we first met – Jamie was thirty-three – and while I wouldn't say that sparks instantly flew, there was definitely a little flicker of, well . . . I'm not quite sure what!

It was 2012 and my first day in a new job as a sales rep at a recruitment company in London. I was all wide-eyed and so nervous about working in the big, bright capital city, with no idea that my whole future was right there in that office. It gives me goose bumps when I think back to that now.

I remember walking in and spotting Jamie sitting at his desk. He had a lovely crisp white shirt on and I thought to myself: 'Ooh, that man has a really wide back.' Maybe that's strange? Haha!

I love broad shoulders on a man because having always felt like a big girl, I like the idea of someone making me feel protected and small. So that was an instant tick for me!

When new people started at work, they were placed with different team managers so that they could train you up on various areas of the job. On that first day, I was asked to sit with Jamie for product training.

So there I was sat next to him, just chatting away, and he made a couple of comments that I couldn't quite figure out. I'm always really, really bad with dry jokes – I'm never sure if someone is actually meaning to be funny or not, and I was just sitting there, not sure how to take him.

Do I laugh? Do I nod in a serious manner? Do I just ignore it? It was honestly the most awkward thing.

Jamie is really well spoken and he's confident with it, too. He's always worked in sales so he has all the patter, and here I was, already feeling like a complete fish out of water for wearing these awful clothes because I wasn't 'with it' when it came to the London fashion and style.

The stuff the girls in the office wore, with their gorgeous handbags and shoes, was a whole new ball game to me. As soon as I walked in on that first day, I realised I needed to get a new coat immediately.

Looking back, my coat was terrible, although it was my

pride and joy at the time. It was from a boutique which was really fashionable where I was from. But clearly not so much in London.

It was a quilted Barbour-style beige jacket and it had the boutique branding emblazoned on the back in pink and cream writing. You know, always handy in case anyone wanted to know where they too could pick themselves up such a cracking gem! I also had the matching cream bag with a fluorescent pink keyring on it. Oh, dear God! It makes me cringe when I think of it now.

All the other girls were in their tailored coats or macs and had tattooed eyebrows, and they were always shopping in Zara, which I'd never even heard of before I came to London. I remember thinking Zara was so posh with its paper shopping bags.

I felt as if I needed to tweak things about myself because I just wanted to blend in, and so the first thing I'd thought was: 'OK, maybe I won't wear that coat tomorrow . . .' Reflecting back on it, it's actually made me feel a bit sad that I felt as if I needed to change something about myself in order to fit in, but we all go through that phase, don't we? Well, I'm sure at least most of us do. I wish I could go back and tell that twenty-two-year-old Soph she just needs to believe in herself and carry on doing what she's doing, because things will all come right in the end.

Anyway, after Jamie had gone through all the information with me, he checked if what he'd said made sense and I was like, 'yeah, yeah, yeah', when the truth was, I was petrified that there was no way I was going to manage to remember it all.

I've always been much better at learning things on the job as I go, rather than taking in loads of instructions, and I think he realised that I hadn't been paying enough attention and that everything he'd said had gone in one ear and straight out the other.

He looked at me, as if to say: 'Are you sure, mate?'

Then he gave me a cheeky wink and said: 'All the best.'

What he meant was 'Good luck, because you're absolutely going to need it!', and that's where our little 'all the best' saying comes from. I quickly realised that everyone used it in the office, like a bit of an inside joke, and it's something me and Jamie have just carried on using ever since.

Who'd have thought one day it would become as well-known as it has?

Despite that slightly odd first encounter, I immediately warmed to Jamie and I was looking forward to working with him.

Whenever we went out for office drinks, as one of the team leaders, he would be given the company credit card to pay for everything. He doesn't drink alcohol, which was another reason he was trusted with the card.

On my first night out with them all, I asked him what he was drinking and he said: 'I've just got a Coke.'

I laughed in a 'haha, yeah right' kind of way, not knowing he was actually teetotal and thinking he was doing one of his dry jokes again.

LITTLE SOPH
16TH FEBRUARY 1990

MINI MRS HINCH

MR & MRS HINCHLIFFE
17TH AUGUST 2018

MY BEST FRIEND
MY MR HINCH

He looked at me deadpan and said: 'Taste it then.'

So I tasted it and realised he was telling the truth, which made me feel so stupid. But it wasn't common for people of our age, and it made me find him more and more intriguing.

I couldn't work him out and I quite liked it. I've since found out that he liked me as well, although he definitely never let on. Not at that stage, anyway.

Truth be told, I didn't really drink alcohol either, but I really wanted to join in the fun and look like I was someone who could live this fast-paced London lifestyle, even though I was travelling back home to Essex on the train every night.

So that evening after office hours I had a right old session and – I won't lie – I was falling about all over the place, trying to dance. Even now all these years later, I'm cringing just thinking about it.

Cut to the chase and I ended up being sick in the toilets of the bar with one of the girls from the office holding my hair back. I mean, how classy, right?

I remember coming out of the toilets and trying desperately to style it out, worried that Jamie would know I'd been sick, which of course he absolutely did because it was all in my hair and he was stone-cold sober.

I just thought: 'Oh Soph, what have you done?'

He came over to check I was all right and I was beyond mortified so said I was fine, although he clearly knew I wasn't.

And, weirdly enough, I'd say that was the night that our friendship really started. We developed a working relationship that was based on a lot of flirty banter, or 'flanter' as Jamie likes to call it.

We still have that today. I hope we never ever lose it.

I settled into the job quite quickly and was enjoying it, being on the phone, meeting my targets and getting to grips with the system. Jamie made me feel relaxed whenever we were around each other and the more I spoke to him, the happier I became. Although still nothing felt safer than coming home at the end of each day.

I didn't want to tell him that I liked him because he was quite high up and I definitely never thought he would be interested in a girl like me. I was twenty-two and to me he was this mature, intelligent and successful man in his thirties. We were mates first and foremost and I didn't want to do anything to lose that.

But as we 'flantered' our way through the weeks and months, I found myself looking forward to going into work purely to see Jamie. I used to get my outfit for the next day ready the night before, planning it all with him in mind. I just wanted him to think I looked nice. I'm seriously blushing just writing about it.

After some time had passed, Jamie and I started speaking regularly on the phone in the evenings. He used to cycle the thirteen miles back from central London to his flat every night and he's told me since that he'd arrive home and hope that there was a missed call from me so he could phone me straight back.

I suppose things got more serious between us from then on. He used to send me suggestions of songs to listen to, normally by bands like Boyz II Men – see, I told you he was cheesier than I am!

One day he sent me 'Pretty Wings' by Maxwell, which has the lyrics: 'Your face will be the reason I smile/But I will not see what I cannot have forever/I'll always love you, I hope you feel the same.'

My heart jumped out of my chest. I thought he was trying to tell me something and so I texted him: 'Oh my God, they are such lovely words from you!'

And he messaged me back massively playing it down, saying: 'Um, they're just the lyrics to a song, you know! It's not me singing it.'

Argh, I wanted the ground to swallow me up whole! Why do boys do this to us?

But then he sent me a wink so I knew, really. He just loved to keep me guessing, to keep the mystery alive. He definitely kept me on my toes.

About nine months after we first met, it was Jamie who made the first move when he sent me an email asking if I fancied getting something to eat after work. Obviously I was screaming on the inside but tried to play it cool and sent him back my attempt at a casual reply, saying: 'Yeah, sounds good.'

That evening we left the office, my stomach in knots, and walked along Oxford Street. Jamie told me to pick somewhere to eat, which is how we ended up in Pizza Express because it was the only place I really knew!

I fell in love with him quite quickly after that night. He told me about how much family meant to him and how proud he was of his parents, and he also asked me so much about my life and I could tell he genuinely cared.

I felt like I was floating. I'd never had feelings like that before so I knew this was something different, something really special.

He made me feel so safe all the time.

I loved the way he was committed to his job and was really well respected and well liked in the workplace, having grafted his way up from the bottom, always making sure everyone was happy and had exactly what they needed.

His parents had emigrated when he was twenty-one (they've since moved back to London) and so he'd had to fend for himself from quite a young age, which I believe had the effect of making him very responsible. He didn't drink or smoke and would never be influenced to, despite people always trying to twist his arm and get him to have a pint. He's always been very strong in his own mind and I bloody love that about him.

We only have two wine glasses in the house and they are for if we ever have guests!

I also really admired that he stood on his own two feet

and had his own flat and just kept everything in the office ticking over. Any place with him in it was nicer, happier and more comfortable.

I loved that he was confident but never ever cocky. He never followed the crew or played to the crowd. He wasn't like other blokes. If there was a bit of laddish banter that went too far, he would step in and squash it. Jamie loves having a joke but he instinctively knows when things have crossed a line and he has a very strong sense of right from wrong.

Everyone in that office got on really well and we'd socialise together after work. It was a really tight bunch, so it didn't take very long for the others to spot the connection between me and Jamie. I'd come back to the office after lunch and the girls would be instantly quizzing me: 'Have you just been out for lunch? Who did you go with?'

But I stayed quiet about it. We wanted to make sure that it was going to go somewhere before we went official because otherwise working together would be really difficult. You don't want to have to break up in front of all your colleagues.

We both knew things were getting serious and it was only a few weeks before we admitted to each other we were in love, although me being me, I managed to blurt it out accidentally so it wasn't anything like those romantic, life goal moments you see in the movies.

We were sat up in his bed after watching *Madagascar* (I

know, so random!) and I remember we were laughing about something or other and I completely obliviously said: 'Oh, I do love you.'

I immediately froze. What had I just said? Oh no! It just slipped out!

He said: 'Sorry?'

And there was this pause of what was probably only a split second but it felt like forever. It was pure agony and I wanted the ground to swallow me up.

'I love you too,' he said.

God, the pure relief!

Even now when he says it to me, I get a flutter in my tummy. I know some people say it at the end of every phone call or whenever they leave the house to go anywhere, but Jamie's never done that. I did used to wish he'd say it more often but now I really like that he doesn't. It means that it's never a throwaway comment. When he does say it, it's special. It's always a lovely moment and I feel something.

We managed to keep it quiet at work for a good while and had fun getting to know each other on secret dates after hours and over the weekends. He'd take me to places like Cadbury World in Birmingham, which showed he'd really put some thought into it.

He wanted to take me to places I'd never been to. I used to avoid London like the plague when I was younger because it was so big and intimidating, but he introduced me to the capital city and that made me feel safe. He'd lived in London all his life so it felt like I had my own personal bodyguard-slash-route guide and he really enjoyed showing me everything, which was so cute. There were a couple of times he took me places I'd already been to but I never let on. I couldn't have spoiled his fun.

I think it got to the point at work where it was obvious, and one night after work when we were all on our way to the pub, our sales director just asked us straight out if we were together.

I started blushing which was probably a dead giveaway in itself. When I'm put on the spot, I'm completely hopeless. I never know how to react and so I get all flustered.

But Jamie said: 'Yes, we are. Well, at least I hope we are!'

And that was it, the cat was out of the bag. Everyone was really happy for us and once the initial excitement at the news died down, no one even batted an eyelid. We were just Jamie and Soph, no dramas.

After nine months together, we moved into a rented two-bed flat in Gidea Park, a suburb of London which is out towards Essex. It felt like the next step in our relationship and the hour-and-a-half drive between Jamie's flat in North London and my parents' place in Essex was starting to become a bit much. We thought we'd move in together on a trial basis to see how we got on.

I wasn't really enjoying my job any more. We'd moved offices and having managed to keep my anxiety at bay for a couple of years, I'd started getting the nervous tummy again every morning. Something had to give.

It was actually Jamie who suggested I leave. He said he would support me to do a hairdressing course at college in the evenings, which was something I'd always dreamed of doing, so I handed in my notice and focused on that.

I loved being back at college and met the most amazing group of girls there.

All of us came in at the same level and it felt like there was no competition. I felt completely at ease and those evenings at the college were some of the most fun evenings of my life.

But it also meant I was on my own quite a lot in the day – Gidea Park is a good forty-five-minute drive away from my mum and my sister in Maldon, so I did feel quite lonely at times.

I said earlier on that this was when the Hinching really started for me. My mum came round one day with that bottle of Zoflora and that was it. I was hooked! Knowing that my little flat was clean and tidy made me so happy.

It was around this time that Henry came into our lives and was the start of us creating our little family together. I've always loved animals and I really wanted a dog to love and care for.

Growing up, I had a Schnauzer called Mason and he was my mum's little boy. He was actually called The Boy and he was an amazing dog. He died about nine years ago now and my mum still gets upset about it.

Jamie had never had a dog growing up so he didn't

really know what to expect. But he instantly fell in love with Henry and he couldn't believe how much affection you get from a dog.

Henry is a pedigree. He didn't cost us much by today's standards for a pedigree puppy, but it was a lot to us at the time – but I can honestly say I would have spent ten times that amount for our boy.

Especially now with everything that's happened to rock our world, I find myself needing Henry more than ever. I stroke him and cuddle him and I honestly couldn't get through some days without him there.

After we got Henry, it felt like we were even more committed to each other and Jamie and I knew we wanted to buy a place together. It was the next stepping stone and so we started saving for a house and made a lot of sacrifices to raise the deposit, which meant no nights out or new clothes or trips away. We were paying a fair amount of rent each month, as you do in London, so it was tough to save on top of that, especially with only one wage coming in, but by 2016 we had scraped enough together and we found our perfect house.

You might have heard of it . . .

It was the corner plot on a new development and as soon as I saw the plans, I had a good feeling about it. We ended up buying it off-plan and we finally moved in that summer. As Jamie worked in London, it was me and my mum who would visit the house on site as it was being built. They made us wear hard hats and hi-vis vests for safety, and I remember Mum being excited because she was just so happy I was moving back to our home town.

I will never forget the day we picked up our keys. I can't put into words how incredible that was for us. Such an indescribable feeling.

Henry was just a puppy and he was loving life, running around the garden like a mad thing while me and Jamie ordered in kebabs and sat outside on the patio eating them.

Come to think of it, it wasn't even that warm, but after living in a flat, we were just so thrilled to finally have our own outdoor space. I know a kebab in your back garden doesn't exactly sound like a big deal, but I was so happy that evening and it felt like everything I'd ever wanted was finally falling into place.

Jamie was really keen to start a family, but I didn't feel ready. I was still only in my mid-twenties and wanted to get settled in our home and be married before we thought about children. I've always dreamed of this fairy-tale life I had planned in my head and I wanted to follow it step by step.

Jamie was happy to wait because he understood where I was coming from, and he's always so supportive of me. We'd been in the house for about a year when he pulled out all the stops and asked me to marry him.

He's very romantic. I'm not at all – I get really embarrassed with that kind of stuff – but Jamie could tell you all our little anniversary dates throughout the whole of our relationship. I sometimes have to check the date of our wedding! That's really terrible, isn't it? Funnily enough, my dad is a hopeless romantic and so is Jamie's. In fact, all of the men in our family wear their hearts on their sleeves. I really love that.

Anyway, I guess I shouldn't have been surprised by Jamie's proposal, which was unreal. Talk about being swept off my feet!

I'd actually arranged for all his family to come over that day, but at the last minute he told me there had been a change of plan and we were going to meet them half-way for a pub lunch instead.

I'd Hinched the house from top to bottom and got a load of nice food in for lunch so I was quite annoyed, if I'm honest! I was stomping round, huffing and puffing in a bit of a strop.

We drove to what looked like a random field (which I know now was North Weald Airfield) and Jamie said he'd organised a surprise for our four-year anniversary before we met everyone in the pub. I was even more confused as to what on earth he was playing at, but then a helicopter landed on the field and he told me we were taking a short flight.

I couldn't believe it. I was so excited! I'd never been in a helicopter before.

We flew all over London and it was just amazing. Jamie was pointing out the offices where we'd first met and it was honestly the most incredible thing anyone has ever done for me.

I didn't realise he had another trick up his sleeve. The entire time we'd been enjoying this magical helicopter ride together, Jamie had been sat there with the ring that he was just about to propose to me with stuffed in his boxers. In his actual pants! How he'd managed to keep it in there safely without it falling out while we were walking around, I do not know. It must have been so awkward!

When we landed back in the field, our families were all secretly waiting there for us in the control tower holding up this big 15-foot banner that said: 'Sophie Barker, will you marry me?'

I turned to look at Jamie and he was down on one knee, holding this little ring box. The box even had a light in it so the ring really sparkled when he opened it.

We'd been to Hatton Garden a few months before to get me some earrings as a joint Valentine's and birthday present, and as a joke I pointed out a ring with a double halo and a diamond in the middle and said: 'Wow, that's so beautiful, wink wink.'

He was obviously paying attention because he got it bang on, bless him.

Of course I said yes, crying so hard! I couldn't get my head around the fact that he'd made such an effort and also that everyone else had managed to keep it a secret from me.

The boy did good. So good.

I threw myself into wedding planning with lists and

even a spreadsheet to keep track of all our spending – you know lists are literally my idea of heaven! We set a budget and really stuck to it and I'm still so proud that we only went over by £27!

Whenever we talk about our wedding day on 17 August 2018 at the stunning Gosfield Hall in Essex, it takes us right back and makes us both smile from ear to ear.

We had everyone we loved and cared about under that one roof and I felt like I was in the middle of a fairy tale.

My dress was my idea of The Dream dress – all I ever wanted was my Cinderella moment and I definitely got it. Wearing that showstopper, with its fitted bodice and the fullest of skirts, was the first time in my life that I've ever felt petite and really girly. I got completely lost in it.

When my lovely dad saw me in it, his little girl all ready to go and get married on the biggest day of her life, he broke down in tears. It was a really emotional moment for both of us and I get choked up now just thinking about it.

I've not put my dress on since. It's folded away in the loft at my mum and dad's house. But I do quite like the idea of getting all my friends together one evening for a girls' night in our wedding gowns! That would be hilarious, although I don't know if mine would fit me now because my whole body has changed since having our Ronnie.

My eight bridesmaids looked beautiful in their silvergrey dresses (come on, what other colour scheme was I going to choose?!) and I wore a necklace and earrings from Next and flat laced ballerina shoes instead of heels.

While I very much wanted the Big Day and the whole shebang, I also wanted it to feel very personal to us. So we added little 'Sophie and Jamie' touches throughout, like naming all the tables after Beyoncé songs. The florist where my mum worked provided the flowers and Jamie's very talented and creative sister designed our order of service, table names and place cards.

Jamie's speech really was something else. He said I'd changed him as a person and thanked me for making him a better man and he had me and everyone else in tears.

It felt like I was holding my breath all day, but as Jamie held me in his arms for our first dance to Brian Mc-Knight and Mariah Carey's 'Whenever You Call', I was finally able to let go. It felt like I breathed deeply for the first time in twenty-four hours and I felt safer and more content than I ever had before.

Being married hasn't changed us as a couple although we definitely feel like we're more of a team. And even now I love referring to 'my husband'. It still gives me a little tingle. I have a husband!

Unfortunately for us, after the amazing high of our wedding came a sudden crash. We didn't know it at the time, but our vow to love each other 'in sickness and in health' would come into practice much sooner than we'd expected.

I have a Protein S deficiency and Factor V Leiden blood

condition. What that means is that I am susceptible to clotting, and just before we were due to fly out to the Maldives on our honeymoon, my left leg swelled up to four times the size and I couldn't walk on it, or even stand.

I was blue-lighted to hospital where they discovered I had a large blood clot in my iliac vein.

After your wedding, in a perfect world you're supposed to be caught up in your honeymoon bubble and jetting off to your beautiful holiday destination, but it sadly just wasn't like that for us. I was laid up in a hospital bed and Jamie was there with a bedpan, helping me to wee. How's that for romance, eh?

I wasn't allowed to get up and walk around and my leg was huge.

I had gone from wearing this breathtaking dress and feeling beautiful to looking the worst I've ever looked.

But Jamie wasn't bothered about any of that at all. He's always preferred me in my loungewear and no make-up with my hair piled up anyway.

Even then, sat in a room having had to postpone our honeymoon, he was still making me laugh. I knew that with him there, everything would be OK. It always is. He makes me feel so safe, and he makes me feel like I can get through anything as long as he's by my side.

The doctors put me on intravenous blood thinners but the clot wasn't responding and my leg swelling was getting worse. In the end, they had no choice but to operate, and during the surgery I was given a clot-buster treatment as well as being fitted with three stents to keep the iliac vein open.

It was a scary, stressful time but all the doctors and the nurses were amazing. I can't ever thank them enough. And after a week I was allowed to go home although I'm now on blood thinners for the rest of my life. Luckily, our holiday insurance allowed us to rebook our honeymoon for December and it was heaven on earth – worth every penny that we'd skinted ourselves for to get there!

While we'd been planning our wedding, the Mrs Hinch madness was starting to bubble away in the background and by the time we got married I was on a good few hundred thousand followers. Neither of us had any idea what we were letting ourselves in for, but the fact that Jamie has been there from the very beginning means he understands all this like no one else.

We've gone through it together and he's with me for who I am, regardless of who might know my name now. (Well, actually, technically it was his name first, wasn't it? All the best, Soph.)

Don't get me wrong, we do bicker. I think it would be odd if we didn't. We're like any other couple, but discussing those differences of opinion is what makes a relationship interesting, isn't it?

Sometimes it comes to a head and we might not speak for a few hours, but we always get over it. He tends to make a joke and annoyingly, I can't help but laugh, and then I'll be so cross that he's cracked me! I'll be trying my hardest to hold my mouth together to stop the laughter, but I can't help it.

That's how we've always been and it's one of the things that attracted us to each other in the first place.

We argue very differently. I like a good sulk and can be really stubborn sometimes (shock!) whereas Jamie has forgotten any argument with a click of the fingers. We flirt one minute and then argue the next. That's basically our marriage in a nutshell.

## A Bit More About Us

I know a lot of you really liked the Couples Cards we've worked our way through over the last year or so. With that in mind, I thought it might be fun to answer a few quickfire questions I often get asked about Jamie (his ears will be burning!).

### Our song . . .

'Whenever You Call' by Brian McKnight and Mariah Carey. It was our first dance. If we've ever been getting on each other's nerves, Jamie will whack that on full blast and we can't stay mad at each other. God, he knows which buttons of mine to press!

### Pet names . . .

Just babe. He sometimes calls me bubs, but that's about as far as it goes. We're not big on nicknames.

### Sum Jamie up in three words . . .

Funny, loyal and brave.

### First kiss . . .

It was in London during our third date in a bar near work. Date three – hell, yes, I made him wait!

### Jamie's celebrity crush . . .

Kate Beckinsale.

### Jamie's celebrity lookalike . . .

He gets told he looks like Tom Hardy. Can't see it myself, but I'm happy with that!

### Favourite body parts . . .

He'd say my eyes, I think. I love his hands.

### His favourite food . . .

He loves most things Italian – pizzas and the salads with the posh meats. Antipasti, is it? That's right, isn't it?

## His signature scent . . .

Estée Lauder's Pleasures for Men

## Last word in an argument . . .

Me. Every time. Sorry, Jamie. I love you!

## Your film . . .

We love to watch a movie together, but I'd have to say, as cheesy as it might sound to some, our wedding DVD is the film we love the most. We often sit down and crack that out.

Jamie deciding to take a career break last summer was a huge turning point for me and for us as a family. We're very lucky that his employer offers its employees time off for up to five years. It's up to the director's discretion whether or not you're awarded the break, and you have to have been there for a minimum of five years. Since Jamie had worked there so hard for twelve, we were keeping our fingers crossed his request would be approved. With everything that was happening with Mrs Hinch and also the fact I was about to give birth to Ronnie, it really was a no-brainer for us. I am grateful every day for the fact that being Mrs Hinch earns us a living, which means we are in the position where Jamie can be at home for now.

I was finding myself getting anxious when he was

going to work – he'd be leaving the house at 6 a.m. and not getting back until 7 p.m. – and, call me a wimp, but I feel nervous doing this on my own. It can be lonely and really daunting at times, and Jamie always has my back. No matter what.

When I wake up in the middle of the night and I struggle to breathe, he calms me down. If I've taken on too much, he will step in and say, 'Soph, you need to take a breather.' He's a brilliant emotional support for me. He comes with me to most of my meetings, which I know some people might think is weird, but we are partners in every sense of the word.

From a practical side of things, I physically couldn't do this without him. He helps me with the filming when I need both hands to Hinch and tidy. If I need to shoot some content and reply to emails and go through and reply to my DMs, then Jamie's always here to look after Ronnie.

He is my wingman in what has become an absolute machine that neither of us ever expected and I need him now more than ever. Some people who have a large Instagram account accept a lot more in the way of outside help than I have chosen to. I prefer to keep my circle small because I want to be hands on and personally involved in everything that has my name on it.

Jamie may very well return to work at some point, but for now we want to have this time together as a family to raise our Ronnie together and give building a family business our best shot. This is an amazing opportunity we've been given, and we don't know when it will end, so we just have to make the most of it while we can.

Lots of people tell me there's no way they could work full-time with their partner, but we used to do it back in the day and believe it or not, we're so busy that we're not in each other's faces all day. Between housework, seeing to Ronnie, replying to emails, doing my stories, running to the shops, meetings, calls to my management and walking Henry, sometimes we sit down to dinner and realise that even though we've both been in the same house all day, we feel like we've not seen much of each other.

With Jamie taking a break from work, our income has obviously changed, but I don't look at anything I earn from being Mrs Hinch as 'my' money because I couldn't do this without Jamie. From the day we moved in together, our money has gone into one pot.

Whatever either of us brings in belongs to both of us – when I was at college doing hairdressing, Jamie supported me on just his wage for two and a half years. He looked after the financial side of things the whole time and never made me feel bad or awkward about it, like it was 'his' money. That's just what you do when you're a team, isn't it? You work together, always.

Nothing fazes Jamie. I find the way he can adapt to any situation really attractive. He can be with my friends who are younger than him and fit in no problem or he can sit down with my dad and have a really good conversation putting the world to rights.

I have to admit, though, that I had the same worries I'm sure a lot of partners have after they've given birth. I was concerned about us losing our spark and Jamie not seeing me in the same way as he did before. Let's just say he spent a lot of my labour down 'that' end watching Ronnie being born and I wondered if he was ever going to be able to find me as attractive again after that. But it turns out my worrying was needless as we've actually been the exact opposite. Our relationship is stronger than ever. If I'm randomly sitting there looking at him he'll say: 'Are you flirting with me?' and one thing leads to another and it all starts from there.

As long as you want to rip each other's clothes off more often than you want to rip each other's heads off then you'll be all right.

One thing we're going to do more of now that Ronnie is a bit older is regular date nights. Mum offers to have Ronnie overnight all the time, but I haven't really wanted to let him go. I know it would be a good break for us, though, so we might just take her up on it from time to time.

Me and Jamie have made a promise to each other to make an effort to go to the theatre and have the odd meal out just as a couple. You do need that time together as it's so easy to slip out of the habit of doing it once you have a baby.

The thing is, we do just genuinely love being at home in the happy place we've created here. Our ideal date night would be being on the sofa, Chinese takeaway and a good TV show. Some people like spas or nice hotels, but that's not what we love to do. It's not us.

So while we are very different people, we actually have more in common than I think even we realise. Above everything, we are soulmates and I feel so bloody lucky that we found each other. Imagine if we never ended up working together and never crossed paths? Gosh, I can't bear to think about it.

He is my husband and my best friend but he is also my whole world and my protector. He always has my best interests and my mental health at heart, and he understands me like no other.

And just when I thought I couldn't possibly love him any more . . . along came our Ronnie.

# Five

# Motherhood

My darling Ronnie,

It's hard to put into words just how proud I am to be your mummy. But I'm going to try my best!

The first time I held you in my arms, I knew that I would spend the rest of my life doing everything in my power to keep you safe, happy and loved.

From that moment, nothing else mattered as much to me. Only you.

Sometimes I just stare at you while you sleep and I can't believe that you're here and that you're ours. I still have to pinch myself that me and Daddy made someone so perfect.

I remember bringing you home from hospital when you were just a few hours old and knowing it was the start of a new chapter for our little family. If I'm honest, neither me nor Daddy really knew what we were doing at first. I had all my baby eBayers lined up, ready to go, and I was just hoping I was enough. It all felt a bit scary. We were frightened of getting it wrong (and poor Daddy didn't even have a clue how *to change a nappy!). But you'll be happy to hear he's a pro at it now.*

*You have already taught us so much. You have opened our hearts to feelings we never knew existed and you filled a hole that we didn't even realise we had.*

*I've adored every single minute of watching your little personality develop as the days go by.*

*When you were first born you were so chilled out and laid back – but that didn't last very long! As soon as you found your voice, there was no looking back, and from just a few months old you definitely knew how to tell us exactly what you want. My funny, feisty little man!*

*You're growing up so fast. Your little pointy finger makes me laugh so much. I wonder who you picked that up from! Sometimes I wish time would slow down so I could hold on to these days for as long as possible. It only seems like last week that you were so tiny and new and now you're a proper little boy.*

*But at the same time, I'm so happy to see you growing so big, strong and healthy and meeting all of your milestones. You even enjoy Mummy's cooking. Ha! So I know we must be doing something right.*

*I'm excited for the future to see who you become. I know Daddy can't wait to take you to your first Arsenal game. I can tell you now that you aren't going to have much choice when it comes to which team to support, I'm afraid. Daddy is convinced you're going to be the Gunners' star striker one day – but no pressure!*

*And Grandad will expect Sunderland to be your second team, just to warn you.*

*I'm looking forward to taking you to the zoo and for family days out in the woods, visits to miniature railways, taking you on boats, going on holidays, picnics in the park and watching you running about with your big brother Henry.*

*Sweetheart, I've learned that life won't always be plain sailing and you'll come to find that as you get older. There will be sadness and heartbreak and challenges you'll have to face. There will be times where you'll worry and when things get tough.*

*But I want you to know that whatever happens, Mummy and Daddy will always, always be here for you and we will do everything we possibly can to give you the happiest life ever.*

*The thought of you ever feeling lonely or confused or scared actually hurts my heart.*

*But those challenges? We will help you overcome them. The heartbreaks? We'll get you through them.*

*And sadness? We will hold you tight and make it better. We can get through anything life throws at us, together.*

*Nothing is impossible, everything is fixable and I only hope you always feel that you can tell me or Daddy anything. I am going to be the very best mummy I can, because you deserve nothing less than that, my gorgeous, charming, smiley, happy boy.*

*Be kind, be humble, be polite, work hard and you'll go far. And know that no matter what, you will always be loved.*

*All my love, now and forever,*

*Mummy xx*

Becoming a mum has made me feel more deeply and more intensely than I ever knew was even possible. The love I have for Ronnie is fierce and every time I look at him I think he is absolute perfection.

I've cherished every single milestone – when he rolled over for the first time; the first time he managed to feed himself with his little hand; when he managed enough strength to sit up unaided. Even him learning to stick his tongue out and how he uses his little finger to point at everything made me want to jump for joy!

And when he smiles at me, my whole heart melts. I understand now why a mother's love is different to anything else. You hear people say that, don't you? But I never ever understood it, until now. It's so much more than love.

Having said that, motherhood has also made me more anxious than ever before. You know I was a worrier anyway, but I can honestly say it's on a new level now.

I don't worry so much about the things I used to; the less significant things like making sure the house is clean or getting to places on time. I worry now instead about a whole new Pandora's box of other things and the strength of that worry is a thousand times more powerful.

I think about the future and worry about that. This probably sounds mad, but I even think (and then worry) about Ronnie being a pensioner in an old people's home! What if he's lonely? Will he be looked after and cared for properly? Will they cook him all his favourite meals?

I mean, I know that sounds daft, but that's where my mind wanders to.

I'm hoping it gets easier, but I'm not sure it does. I guess it'll be something I get used to and just have to learn to live with.

It's non-stop, though, isn't it, being a parent? I can't keep up with all the learning! Just when you think you've got a handle on something and you can do it with your eyes shut, along comes a great big curveball to throw you off track again.

That's parenting in a nutshell, I've come to realise.

Jamie and I had always planned to start a family as soon as we were married. I'd had the coil in for years but got it removed a few months before the wedding, hoping I could get pregnant quickly. Neither of us drink alcohol so I wasn't bothered about not being able to have a glass of champagne at the wedding or a cocktail on our honeymoon.

So we'd actually been trying for a little while before the wedding itself and when it didn't happen straightaway, I started to panic. I tried to focus on the wedding rather than getting pregnant, but it was troubling me.

What if I couldn't have children? I knew how much Jamie wanted to be a dad – what if I couldn't give him the one thing I knew was so important to him?

I'd never had any medical concerns that would affect my fertility, and my periods have always been very regular, but it was nagging away at me. Everything was going so well – finding Jamie, getting Henry, buying our house and having the dream wedding – so I was waiting for something to go wrong just like I always do.

I know now it was my anxiety rearing its ugly head again and convincing me that surely something had to rock this boat because everything seemed like it was going too well . . .

However, after being in hospital with the blood clot in my leg following the wedding, we actually decided to put the baby plans on hold for a year because of the stents I'd had fitted in my iliac vein. They recommend you give the stents a chance to settle in, as carrying a baby can sometimes put a lot of pressure on them. We were advised that it wasn't a good idea for me to get pregnant for the time being and so I put it to the back of my mind and we carried on as normal thinking it was something for the future. Just a month later, one evening in October, I went round to my mum's house for a cup of tea and she seemed oddly concerned about how I was behaving. I said I felt a bit tired so was planning on going home and curling up on the sofa for the evening.

She looked at me straight in the eye and said: 'Do a pregnancy test, Soph.'

I laughed and told her I knew I wasn't pregnant because I'd just had my period.

Mum raised an eyebrow and said: 'OK, I'll see you tomorrow . . .'

I went home and I couldn't get what she'd said out of my head, so I thought, 'OK, I'll do it', and I got a test from the bathroom cabinet.

A few minutes later I was sitting there staring at the

word 'pregnant' on the digital screen. I couldn't believe my mum knew before even I did!

What I did next sounds crazy, but you have to understand I was in a state of complete and utter shock. It was nearly midnight but I bypassed Jamie in the lounge, got straight in the car and went back to my mum's house. I knocked on the door but she was in bed, so I called the house phone.

She eventually opened the door, her eyes still half shut, and she let me inside.

'Come in,' she said, putting her arm around me. 'I was right, wasn't I?'

'How did you know, Mum?'

'Your face, kidda. There was something different, something I'd seen in your sister when she was pregnant.'

I was just shaking. My head was all over the place. Obviously first and foremost, I was over the moon. But then, as I always do, my head went straight to the worry side of things, and remembered I had my book coming out and signings lined up all over the country and the thought of possibly having to let people down made me feel absolutely awful.

My mum told me to calm down, and that it would be OK, we'd work everything out and that everyone would be delighted for me.

And then I suddenly realised: I hadn't even told Jamie!

So I got back in the car, drove home and handed Jamie the positive test. I don't think he'd even noticed I'd gone back out! He looked at the test, looked back at me and then burst into tears.

'WE'RE HAVING A BABY!' he cried.

Neither of us had had a clue because we'd stopped focusing on trying.

Mind, they do say when you stop actively thinking about it, that's often when it tends to happen, so maybe that's what it was!

My nerves about telling my management, who were helping me plan my book tour at the time, turned out to be completely needless. Everyone was so happy for us. Even my consultant at St Thomas' who advised me post-clot to hang fire on getting pregnant seemed pleased, and I told him that I was going to do everything I could to keep myself as healthy as possible during the pregnancy.

Jamie became even more protective over me and just seemed to smile whenever he looked at me. I'd be sitting there and I'd catch him just looking at me being pregnant. He's always made me feel really protected and cared for because that's what I need and crave – someone to reassure me that everything is going to be OK.

But now I was seeing a whole new side to him, a really strong side, and I knew our baby was going to have the best dad in the world. It felt so right.

I always wanted to find out whether we were having a little boy or a little girl. Jamie wasn't bothered either way, but I couldn't stop myself. I do quite like the idea of keeping it a surprise for the next one, but when it comes to it I know deep down that I won't be able to resist. I'm too impatient and I like to plan!

We went for the gender scan and the sonographer wrote down the sex and put it in a sealed envelope. We weren't sure what to do with it, but one of my friends popped round for a cuppa after work and I gave her the still-sealed envelope.

'Kid,' I said to her, 'I need you to open this in private and then get a cardboard box and put a boy or girl balloon in it. Come back when you can!'

That was it. She was on a one-woman mission!

'Leave it with me,' she replied and off she drove, the only person who knew whether we were having a boy or a girl.

She came back round that evening with this box and handed it to us. I felt so nervous.

Jamie and I sat on the sofa and opened the lid to find a little 'baby boy' balloon and we both just fell into each other's arms, overcome with emotion.

I put the video of us finding out on my stories and the reaction was incredible.

Of course I would have been happy either way, but if I could have chosen, it would have been a boy. I'd been suffering with a lot of morning sickness and so I was convinced it was a girl, as the old wives' tale goes. So it was even more of a surprise.

I was just thinking 'That's my boy!' and I wanted to be everything I could be for this little man growing inside me.

The sickness was bad for about four months, but I

was almost happy to feel that because it was a sign I was pregnant.

The second trimester was amazing. I was healthy, doing a lot of Hinching and felt on top of everything I needed to. I was doing a lot of nesting and loved getting my hospital bag ready and interacting with and taking advice from my Hinchers – you guys always know best! Getting the bag ready was one of my favourite parts of being pregnant, working out what I needed, what Ronnie would need, finding baby eBayers and getting excited for the day he would be here.

If you're about to have a baby, I'm wishing you all the love and luck in the world! I get a lot of questions about what I took in my hospital bag so I thought I'd pop a list here. Here's what I would recommend:

### How to Hinch your Hospital Bag

Clear toilet bags so you can see all your beauty bits easily

Handheld fan

Flipflops for the hospital shower

Straws so you can sip liquids easily while in labour

Lip balm

Your favourite butter so when you have that first slice of toast it feels like home!

PJs, but make sure they are dark – you will be leaking a lot of bodily fluids (sorry)

Big massive maternity pads

Huge granny knickers (I still wear mine now – so comfy!)

Cereal bars

Haribo. Lots of Haribo.

'First photo' card – I nearly forgot this!

Fluffy socks

Dry shampoo

Little bag for dirty laundry

Sandwich bags with full baby outfits inside so you're not rummaging around trying to find a pair of socks

Baby essentials, like newborn-sized nappies, cotton wool and nappy cream

After really enjoying that middle part of my pregnancy, it was the final stages where it all went south.

I was seven months gone and had a rare day at home as it was slap bang in the middle of my book tour. I'd just come in from the garden to the lounge when I had this horrendous attack of pain in my lower back and groin.

I don't know where it came from, but I fell to the floor in agony and managed to pull myself along to the downstairs loo on my elbows. I found myself grabbing the toilet bowl and screaming in pain. Unbearable, awful pain. I thought the baby was coming, that's how bad it was.

Jamie came rushing through in a panic and called an

ambulance and my mum. They took me straight to Broom-field Hospital and I had another attack in there. It actually happened four times across the three days I was in there and no one has ever been able to give me an explanation for it. Maybe it was my bones moving into position pre-paring for the baby, but it honestly felt like they were all breaking. I don't know why, but it was more painful than Ronnie's actual birth itself.

If anyone has experienced anything similar, I'd love to know, because it's still a mystery to me.

I have to be thankful that happened, though, because while the doctors were investigating the possible cause, they discovered another complication, unconnected to the attacks but potentially far more dangerous.

As many of you will already know, in 2011 I'd had a gastric band fitted that helped me to lose eight stone but also caused a series of health issues.

I'm going to talk about my experience with this in greater detail later on in the book, but if I'd known how one operation would turn into such a hideous nightmare lasting the best part of a decade, I would never have gone through with it.

By the time I was pregnant, the band had previously been unclipped so was no longer working. As Ronnie grew and my stomach got bigger, the band moved and it caused what the doctors described as something similar to a kink in a hosepipe.

Basically, no food could go down into my stomach and

whatever nutrients were going in from liquids, Ronnie was taking through the placenta.

The baby will always take what they need, so as a result I was losing weight – I was 8 stone 5 pounds at seven months pregnant, which is frighteningly underweight for my 5-foot 10-inch frame.

I was getting a lot of hurtful comments at the time for appearing malnourished and thin, looking like a stick or a 'skinny rat' as someone so kindly put it, but people didn't know what was really going on. I wasn't dieting. I would never do that. Of course I would never put the health of my baby at risk. I wanted to put on weight so badly and was eating soups, protein shakes, ice cream and absolutely anything soft and easy and full of calories that I could manage. Thankfully, Ronnie was growing fine, and that was what I was most concerned about. I had lots of growth scans for him and had his heart monitored regularly and he was always really strong.

I was the one who had been getting weaker.

The doctors at Broomfield fitted me with a feeding tube in order to get more calories into me but I was desperate to finish the last three dates of my book tour. So much so that I pulled the tube out and went to check myself out of hospital to get on the plane to Glasgow.

I desperately didn't want to disappoint any of my Hinchers who I was so looking forward to seeing, and who I knew were all looking forward to seeing me. It was Jamie who put his foot down. He very rarely gets like that with me; he's normally very soft. But he said very firmly: 'No. You stay on that bed.'

He called my management for back-up because I was digging my heels in, but little did I know that they had already cancelled all of the remaining tours, as there was absolutely no way they were going to let me go being as poorly as I was. Everyone had been telling me from the start that I was crazy to want to still do the tours, but I really didn't want to let anyone down. They were all on the same page and I was officially outnumbered.

I still feel dreadful about that and I'm so sorry to the Hinchers who felt let down, but it was the right thing to do because the next thing we were told was that I would have to have an operation under general anaesthetic.

The band was inactive but it needed to be moved. If you think of it as being like a belt still threaded through the loop of your jeans when they're undone, when you fold your jeans up, the belt gets in the way, doesn't it? So my Ronnie bump was pushing upwards and the gastric band was causing a blockage which could only be 'unkinked' with surgery. Honestly, I was devastated.

I got rushed from Broomfield to St Thomas's in London and going down to theatre was the scariest thing I've ever done.

General anaesthetic while pregnant has a risk of bringing on an early birth, so my mum went out and bought a load of tiny baby grows just in case he had to come early. Even though it felt like I'd been pregnant forever, I knew it was too soon. He couldn't come yet, he needed to stay in there where he still had some growing to do, and was safe.

I was shaking and sweating, not out of worry for myself but out of fear for our boy, and as I was being put to sleep, I held on to my stomach thinking: 'Please, please, just let him be OK.'

Thankfully, the surgery went well but when I came round, it wasn't a slow process of coming back into the room. Instead, I bolted straight up. God knows what that did to my stitches! But I didn't care. I didn't even care how the operation had gone. All I cared about was my baby.

The midwife put the Doppler on my stomach to find his heartbeat and I'll never forget the moment she gently said: 'I can hear him. He's there.'

I broke down. That was when I realised how being a mother is the most amazing but also the most terrifying thing in the world and I know I'm going to have heart-stopping experiences like that for the rest of my life. The thought of Ronnie ever being hurt or in pain or not being here is just too much to bear.

I ended up staying in for ten days and had the general anaesthetic plus three blood transfusions without any of my followers knowing. I didn't want to be one of those people trying to get sympathy while on a drip in hospital and with my phone in my face, so I put on my big girl pants and had a laugh with my Hinchers instead. And even whacked Gretel out a couple of times from my hospital bed.

People asked what was wrong, but I didn't say anything

about why I was in there other than it was just a check-up on baby and we were both fine. I knew there were people with far worse to deal with and I didn't want to worry them with my own concerns, but it was a very tough time. Ronnie was always completely fine; it was *my* health that was touch and go. But when they said I needed to stop worrying about the baby and start worrying about myself, I couldn't separate the two. Ronnie was me and I was him. I remember the media wanting exclusives about why I was in hospital too, but that was the last thing I was interested in.

We eventually got home and I was under strict instructions to take it easy for the rest of my pregnancy. And for all the complications I had in that last trimester, my birth was absolute textbook.

My hips are quite narrow – I don't have those child-bearing curves you hear about – so I was convinced I wouldn't be able to give birth naturally.

Given my medical history and blood condition, my pregnancy was consultancy-led and I was always going to have Ronnie at St Thomas's where they had all my bloods ready in case anything went wrong.

They allowed me to get to thirty-seven weeks, which is regarded as full-term, and then brought me in to be induced because they wanted me to give birth in a controlled environment rather than risking me going into natural labour.

I would have loved to have had a water birth, but it was never going to happen that way and I accepted that I had to go with what the team advised. Whatever it took, I just needed to get through it.

In the morning they gave me a pessary, which softens the cervix and would hopefully kick-start labour, but nothing happened. We were sitting twiddling our thumbs until about 11 p.m. when they decided to try the next stage of induction, which was inserting a prostaglandin gel with a syringe and told us that could take another twenty-four hours.

My mum, sister and Jamie were all there and as it was midnight by then, they headed back to a nearby hotel and the midwife said they'd let them know if anything happened.

It was actually only a few hours later at 2 a.m. that they had to come rushing back! I'd gone to the toilet and seen that my wee was pink which automatically made me panic I was losing the baby, but it was actually my waters breaking. I'd always assumed it would look like, well, water! But being a first-time mum there were loads of things I was quite clueless about.

With Ronnie's head sitting so low, they hadn't been able to tell how far dilated I was and so I was a lot further on than they'd thought. That meant there was no time for any pain relief and it all happened very quickly from there in the end.

The contractions started coming thick and fast. The worst part was getting through one and knowing there was another coming straight after and I'd scream through each one.

The gas and air didn't touch the sides, mate! It actually made me feel sick more than anything.

I had my sister, my mum and Jamie in the room with me. I know that set-up wouldn't be everybody's preference, but I needed them. There was no way I was having my baby without all three of them there.

For some reason it was my sister who I felt I needed the most. I was constantly looking for her and kept saying I couldn't do it.

'But, Soph,' she'd say, 'you ARE doing it!'

You think that your body is going to give in but it doesn't, it somehow just keeps going.

Jamie was mopping my face with a wet cloth which was drenched in my sweat rather than cooling water, and one of the midwives was holding one of my legs because I kept on kicking out.

Eventually she said to Jamie: 'You're going to have to hold your wife's leg because she's too strong for me and I can't keep it still!'

My mum came over at that point and held my face firmly in her hands and made me look straight at her.

'Now you listen to me,' she said, in the no-nonsense tone I've known my whole life.

'You need to do this. You can do this. Breathe and listen to what the midwives are telling you.'

I was twenty-nine years of age, in the middle of labour, about to become a mother myself and getting told off! It just goes to show there's no situation where you can't get a dressing-down by your mum.

I remember the midwife telling me to give it one last big push and that was it. After just two hours of labour and a few excruciating pushes, Ronnie was born and they put him straight on my chest, all 6 pounds 1 ounce of him.

For some reason, I couldn't look down. I remember staring at these white cupboard doors ahead of me and being aware of this warm head on my chest but being too scared to look at my baby. I was physically shaking.

Jamie cut the umbilical cord while I was still in shock and I've got a photo of us at that moment. My sister took so many pictures and they are brutal but beautiful!

Some of them I'm a bit like 'What the hell is *that*?' Legs akimbo, the cord still hanging out and so graphic they make you cringe. They're very personal photos and I'd say that I'm pleased we've got them, but, jeez!

When I finally worked up the courage to gaze down at Ronnie, he looked like he was covered in a load of margarine. I know it's naive but I thought he'd come out all pink and lovely and he was actually covered in what looked like Flora! And the cord was this huge, bright blue snake – the size of it blew my mind.

I couldn't believe how much of an image he was of Jamie – they are two peas in a pod, even down to the shape of their eyelids. We've recently been looking through some of my old baby pictures and there's definitely some of me in him, but overall he's his father's son, all right.

I was dripping with sweat but it was a relief to know there was no more pushing. They took him, weighed him and popped a little hat on him and I tried to let everything sink in.

When they brought him back to us, Jamie had skin-to-skin and that's the first time in my life I can say I felt really proud of myself.

'They're my boys,' I thought. 'My gorgeous boys.' I couldn't wait to start our new life together.

But I'm not going to lie, what I also wanted was a shower! I was so sticky and felt pretty grim and desperately needed a wash and so my sister and my mum helped me to the cubicle and basically hosed me down while I gripped on to the handrail. I must have looked a right sorry sight, but you leave your inhibitions at the door when you give birth. I felt a lot better once I was cleaned up, but bloody hell, the reality of childbirth is beyond harsh.

You know you hear about the first post-labour cup of tea and slice of toast and how amazing they taste? That's all well and good, but oh my God, why does no one tell you about the first wee?! I was howling with the pain.

I'd had three stitches after the birth so it was intense, and I was so traumatised that I didn't want to have to go to the toilet ever again!

My mum said next time I needed to go, to put some cool water in a cup and to physically slosh myself as I was weeing, which I did, and that helped.

Apologies for the mental image I've just given you there, but I'd definitely advise all post-partum new mums to have that special wee cup at the ready!

After packing a hospital bag big enough for a week-long stay (you know I like to be prepared!), we actually went home mid-afternoon the same day. In, out, no messing about.

Being at home that first night was so nerve-wracking. I didn't dare go to bed because I didn't know what to expect. I was overwhelmed by what lay ahead and the reality that this was our life now. I think most new mums will relate to those first nights of just feeling disorientated. It's like you're shell-shocked.

Jamie is the sort of person who always declares that everything is fine and likes to fix things and make them better. So his bright idea was to tell me to go up to bed to catch up on sleep and that he would stay downstairs and look after Ronnie.

I'm not joking, at that point he hadn't even changed a nappy. And there was no way I was leaving our baby on the first night! And thank God I didn't, because, bless him, we soon realised that Jamie actually couldn't change a nappy to save his life.

It was when Ronnie was a couple of months old and we were looking back to that first night that Jamie finally admitted he didn't know what he'd been thinking. He couldn't believe he'd even suggested it.

I asked him what he would have done and he said he'd have had to call me back downstairs after ten minutes. So that would have been a successful 'catch up on sleep' . . .

But he shouldn't feel embarrassed of that because it came from a good place. I just want dads and mums to know there's no shame in admitting you haven't got a clue what you're doing. Nobody does! All new parents have to start somewhere and learn together.

Jamie found it hard accepting that for once in his life he didn't have it all in the bag and he wasn't able to make everything OK. He struggled being dropped in the deep end at first. We both did.

I wish I'd been able to take in more of those first few days. My mum was a rock and helped us with everything, including things like how to change a nappy while battling with the belly peg where the cord had been clipped.

I remember it felt strange calling him Ronnie, like it made it seem too real, and we actually called him Jiminy for the first few days because he looked like Jiminy Cricket from *Pinocchio*. After a few days we knew we had to start calling him Ronnie before we got too used to Jiminy and it stuck!

I really wanted to give breastfeeding a go because it's natural and I knew it had lots of benefits for the baby and was great for bonding, and luckily, Ronnie was so clever with it. He found the boob by himself shortly after he was born, latched straight on and took to it really well. It hurt at first and so I expressed as well as breastfeeding in order to give my nipples a bit of a break.

I hadn't realised that the first milk, which I now know is called the colostrum, is orangey, thick and creamy. When I first saw it, I thought my milk was infected! I freaked out.

But Mum smiled at me and explained it was just what you produced for the first few days until your proper milk comes in and it had everything that Ronnie needed. The colostrum is packed with antibodies and I feel good that he had every drop I produced.

I really tried to persevere with the breastfeeding, but my confidence was knocked when Ronnie lost a bit of weight at the beginning and I felt like a complete failure.

I know now that it's very common for babies to lose weight at first, but all I could see was that he'd gone down to 5 pounds 10 ounces and I felt so embarrassed.

I thought: 'What have I done wrong?'

We started topping up with a bit of formula and did a combination of bottle and breast for the next few weeks. But I kept doubting my ability to breastfeed at all and it started to play on my mind not being able to see how much he was taking.

At least with the bottles I could see the amount he'd had and in my head that made things better. I felt a lot of pressure to continue, mainly from myself, to be honest, but also from a few online advisers who were saying I needed to make sure I breastfed him.

After a few weeks, the health visitor told me it was OK to stop breastfeeding if I wanted to. It was like she was giving me permission to stop and I think that was what I needed to hear. And so I decided to move completely to bottles and it felt like a weight had been lifted.

I'm so pleased I got to experience it and am very grateful that Ronnie had my milk. I wish I'd been able to do it for longer, though, and stopping sooner than I'd have liked was something I really did have to come to terms with.

For my next baby I hopefully won't be as anxious and I'll have a bit more knowledge and experience behind me, so I definitely want to try and carry on for longer.

Stopping breastfeeding eased the stress a little bit, but the mental situation I was finding myself trapped in was far greater than just one issue and I was starting to seriously struggle.

Before you have a baby you imagine being in this magical bubble, but the truth is, you're also very on edge and exhausted and a newborn changes everything, bringing an incredible amount of stress to any relationship.

Add in the raging hormones, anxiety and trying to recover from giving birth, and I definitely lost myself for a little while and it was really quite scary.

I was also trying to come to terms with the fact that my whole body looked different. I looked in the mirror and didn't know who I was. I genuinely didn't recognise who was looking back at me and with these huge, milk-filled boobs and a body I wasn't used to, I felt like a different person.

And then I'd hear Ronnie's cry and think: 'That's my baby. I can't believe that's my baby.'

It was as if it was all happening to someone else.

I'd hesitate before labelling what I went through as postnatal depression. Quite honestly, I'm not entirely sure.

But one million per cent, I showed a lot of the signs. I felt guilty for feeling so down when I should have been happy and grateful to have had a healthy baby. Many people aren't as lucky and Ronnie was a planned and very much wanted baby, so why couldn't I lift myself out of this lowness I was feeling?

I found myself waking up some mornings with my stomach feeling like it had dropped. I couldn't manage the everyday routine – the things you do without think-ing, like getting dressed and making breakfast, became almost impossible.

I remember Ronnie started refusing his milk for a cou-ple of days and I told myself he wasn't drinking it because it was me who was feeding it to him. I looked at his eyes and felt like I wasn't making him happy enough. It broke my heart.

I already felt awful that I hadn't been able to con-tinue breastfeeding and now this was happening with the bottle and he was going to starve and it was all my fault.

I love Ronnie so much, but knowing his whole survival depended on me felt like a huge pressure. And I couldn't help worrying that he could have a better life if it wasn't me who was his mummy. If he had someone who knew what they were doing, maybe he would be happier.

Looking back, I know now that those thoughts were irrational and over the top, but that's how I was feeling at the time. I was on a hormonal rollercoaster and I just couldn't help it.

Jamie struggled to understand at first. He'd say it was OK, not to worry, and would try and find the right words to calm me down.

He'd point out all the positives: 'Look at how he's smiling and looking around and cooing.'

But words couldn't help, really. You can't just snap out of it because the mind doesn't work like that.

The midwife came to see me, and my mum, who knew I was finding it tough, said she would take Ronnie into the garden while we had a chat.

I just broke down in tears and poured my heart out about how depressed I was feeling. The midwife suggested going to the doctor's and said I could maybe have a think about getting something prescribed that could pick me up. I know I should have followed her advice, but

I felt better for having spoken about it with her and so I left it, thinking everything would be OK now.

But after a couple of days things weren't OK again and I started spiralling.

We were having the extension built (I know, I know, a new baby plus house renovations are never an ideal combination!) and I was paranoid about the paparazzi being outside the house after I'd spotted one in a van with a long lens at the end of the road.

That's when we decided to pack up and leave Essex for a few weeks so we could get away from the mess and the noise in the house and all the other pressures of being at home.

The four of us – me, Jamie, Ronnie and Henry – spent the next few weeks staying in the Suffolk countryside, moving around different cottages and lodges. I came off Instagram and spent some of my time walking out in the fields. Knowing that no one knew I was there was so freeing and therapeutic, but my anxiety levels around Ronnie didn't seem to be getting better.

My management was worried I was going to become seriously ill and so recommended a therapist who helps with a lot of people in the public eye. I spoke to her on FaceTime for a good few hour-long sessions and she was so lovely. It really helped to just speak to someone neutral about everything I was feeling.

She had a very soothing voice. She sounded a little bit

like a satnav, actually! In a way, that makes sense, because she was literally navigating me through life. Like, turn left here! Straight on! Take a right!

I wish I'd carried on with it longer because, looking back now, I can see that it was starting to help and I don't think I gave it enough of a chance. I can get quite impatient when I don't see instant results, and I wanted a quick fix to make it all go away. I just wanted to go back to feeling like my old self again.

Of course, when it comes to mental health, there is no such thing. It would be lovely if there was.

I just couldn't see myself ever feeling relaxed again. Is he sleeping OK? Is his bag packed to go out? Does he need feeding? Is his nappy changed? Is he too hot? Too cold? You feel like the whole rest of your life you're going to be anxious about something and it can feel exhausting.

It was putting a strain on my relationship with Jamie and things came to a head with the two of us when Ronnie was eight weeks old. I think the two-month mark is where it really hits you. This is real life now, no going back.

We'd not long arrived back from Suffolk and Jamie had taken Henry out for a walk while I was trying to get Ronnie to sleep. I was lying on the bed and he was in his Next2Me crib and I just found myself uncontrollably crying. Sobbing and sobbing, weeping into my pillow. I don't know what had started it but I was distraught.

Jamie came back and instead of asking me what was

wrong and checking I was OK, he looked at me and said: 'You're acting crazy.'

He made me feel like I'd lost my marbles and I suddenly felt a huge rush of anger.

'Don't EVER use that word!' I shouted.

'Well, why are you crying?'

'I don't know why I'm crying myself, Jamie! Let alone being in a position to explain it to you!'

And I collapsed back on the bed, my whole body heaving with sobs.

Jamie very rarely says anything that upsets or hurts me, but that really stung. It felt like a kick to the gut.

He put his arms around me and apologised.

'I'm so sorry, babe,' he said. 'I didn't realise that would touch a nerve.'

I told him to go away and read up on postnatal depression and post pregnancy mental health.

And you know what? That's exactly what he did. I'm so proud of him that he did that – I'm not sure all men would have bothered. And he soon realised why that throwaway comment really hurt me.

That row was a low point but also a turning point for us. Jamie started to understand how seriously this was affecting me and that I couldn't control how I was feeling, and he was so much more patient with me.

I could be laughing one minute and then crying the next, and it didn't make me crazy. I could be nervous about something but also excited. Swinging between different emotions was normal and once I felt Jamie understood me, I started to feel more relaxed and supported.

We started to talk more honestly about exactly how we were both feeling.

We had been trying without any success to get Ronnie into a routine, but I found it was putting even more pressure on top of an already stressful situation. When he wasn't sleeping at the time it was supposed to be bedtime, I'd think I'd done something wrong and would go back over all my actions to determine what wasn't working. That was so tiring and ultimately pointless.

I do understand that some babies respond well to routine, but for us it worked better to let it happen naturally rather than forcing it.

Ronnie found his own routine. We all did.

When I accepted that I wasn't failing when something didn't go according to 'The Plan', that's when I could enjoy things more.

I also got rid of the baby apps. I had downloaded one of those apps that tells you about what behaviours and developments to expect based on your baby's age, hoping it would help me feel more prepared. But it ended up just making me feel more anxious and overwhelmed about what was to come. I had to delete them in the end.

Those apps might work for some people, but they were making me worse and I decided I had to go with the flow a bit more.

I don't see how one size can fit all when it comes to little ones. They are all individuals and what works for one won't necessarily work for another.

For that reason, I couldn't look at baby books, either. Again, it worked better for me to figure things out on my own. My mum had bought me a book when I was pregnant called *What to Expect When You're Expecting* and I'd found that really helpful because it felt like someone was talking to me all the time, like I was having a conversation with a book.

But after I had Ronnie I couldn't do it. It's great that some people are helped by the books but it wasn't for me.

Everyone is different, all babies are different.

I'd also tell myself: 'He's OK and he loves you.' And the more I said it, the more I believed it.

Time was by far the biggest healer. As the weeks went on, I slowly but surely started to feel a lot better; more myself. I had an amazing support network and as I'm the last one of my friends to have a baby, I always have brilliant advice available to me. I never felt alone and I'm so grateful for that.

Ronnie is lucky to be in this little family and I know that now. He is loved and safe and we have a lovely life all together. But those difficult early weeks clouded a lot of the happy times and I wish I'd been able to enjoy them a bit more. Next time I hope I will.

Finding out that I'd been voted on to *Mother & Baby*'s

2020 Mum List was the most incredible feeling. I've won other awards before, but none of them felt quite the same as this one. Knowing that people had voted for me and had been inspired by my journey as a mummy is just indescribable and it made me feel like I'd finally been accepted into the 'mum' community. It took me a long time to feel part of that, mostly because of my own self-doubts and lack of confidence. So thank you, to every single one of you who took the time to nominate me. It really does mean the world.

I don't know everything, but I'm not afraid to ask for advice and I've learned so much, not just about how to physically look after our baby but also about relationships and how important good communication is.

We were guests on a podcast last year and Jamie, God love him, said he thought he was 'useless' when Ronnie was first born and that shocked me. I felt so sad for him.

I knew he wasn't the most experienced when it came to babies, but I never ever thought he was useless and I wish he'd told me that's how he was feeling. No, he didn't know the basics, but he picked them up so quickly and when he holds Ronnie now, I am amazed at how far he's come. And the way Ronnie looks at him . . . it's pure love and adoration.

It's OK to admit to each other that you don't know. It's not a competition about who is the most tired, or a game of one-upmanship. Just understand each other and empathise and treat it as teamwork. When one of you flops, the other should be there to pick things up.

Becoming parents is not like it is in the movies. Sometimes you sit there so knackered that your whole body aches and you think that even if you put your head down on a brick you would sleep. That tiredness puts pressure on even the most solid of relationships and things that wouldn't normally bother you suddenly become the cause of ridiculous rows.

I remember getting really irritated one morning by Jamie clinking his cereal bowl with his spoon. I blew up at him but then thought: 'Why am I getting annoyed about that?'

We can laugh about it now, but when you're in the thick of it, you can't think straight.

It changes your relationship forever, but in our case, thankfully, it's been for the better and we're also closer than we've ever been. Both of us really salute single parents who do what they do on their own. I have so much respect for them. How single mums and dads cope I do not know; they are all heroes.

Something Jamie and I worked very hard on, and were determined to get right, was the relationship between Ronnie and Henry. It was so important that the two of them bonded early on and so we'd have them together every morning on the bed with me there the whole time.

The connection they have is even stronger than I hoped for. I totally see them as brothers!

But even now they are never left on their own together because you just don't ever know and it's not worth the risk. Ronnie is very inquisitive and he can sometimes pull Henry's fur, so I make sure that Ronnie knows that he is not to do that. And I make sure Henry knows he's not to lick Ronnie's face. Henry needs to know there are boundaries too.

But I feel the love between them and I feel safe when they're around each other.

Both Jamie and I are very aware that thanks to the success of Mrs Hinch and our growing business, Ronnie is lucky enough to have a comfortable upbringing. Even so, we will make sure that he always knows the value of money and the importance of working hard, meeting deadlines, getting up in the morning and having a purpose in life.

We both had that drilled into us early on and have worked ever since we were able to – Jamie had a paper round from a young age and I washed pots in the local pub – and Ronnie will be no different.

He will have Saturday jobs and holiday jobs just like we did. Jamie's dad was a car salesman, but Jamie still had to go out and earn the money to buy his own car.

I'd love Ronnie to be in a position to help grow our family business one day, but he'd need to work hard to get there and there won't be a silver spoon in sight. He will have to prove himself, because it's not going to be handed to him on a plate.

Obviously, I don't want him to feel like he has to worry about money, but if he wants a new top-of-the-range phone when his old one is working perfectly fine, it's not happening. That's how I've been brought up.

If he wants something, he can wait for Christmas and birthdays like we had to.

I often wonder what I did with my days before Ronnie. It's almost hard to remember a life before him. Sometimes me and Jamie ask each other what we used to talk about, because these days even when he's asleep, the only topic of conversation is Ronnie and looking at photos of him!

He is our whole world. The parenting police on social media say I shouldn't be holding and cuddling him to sleep and that he should be going straight down. But I think there's going to be a time when he doesn't want to be cuddled and so I'm going to make the most of it while I can.

I love rocking him and staring at him fast asleep in my arms. I have to fight the urge to eat his little edible cheeks! And his random little tuft of hair at the side has become such an obsession of mine that it often moves me to tears. I can't cope with the cuteness. Little tufters.

He's growing up so fast I often want to press the pause button. Sometimes it feels like time is flying away before we've had a real chance to appreciate each amazing stage.

But I'm also really excited about what's coming next, because I can't wait to see more of the little boy he's turning out to be and I feel like we've come so far as a family. I've coped with the pressures of being in the public eye, having the extension done, pregnancy, birth and motherhood, and I've realised I can manage more than I thought I could. I really need to stop doubting myself so much, because that's a lot to contend with and we came through all of it.

And to all the people bringing up little ones out there, I'd like to say this. It's OK to have good and bad days. It's normal to feel like you're getting it wrong. Don't feel guilty if you're finding it tough. We all do.

You're never alone, so talk about how you're feeling, own it, ask for support if you need it and don't be too proud to accept the offers of help. It's mind-blowing what a second pair of hands can do.

Take advice from a few trusted sources – your mum, your best friend, your health visitor – and ignore the busy-bodies who will say you're doing it wrong, whatever it is. We can't all be perfect like them, can we?

Oh, and keep a memory box and scrapbooks! I've kept all Ronnie's hospital bands, the clip from the cord, his first pair of socks, his first baby grows, his first little Arsenal kit and his first dummy. I've also got a scrapbook I've been filling in from the start of my pregnancy, which I've loved. I love looking back through all of those keepsakes, so I'd totally recommend doing this.

Finally, cuddle your babies as much as you can. Kiss

them, squeeze them, hold them, and never ever be made to feel bad about that.

Mothers are warriors and we've got this. We are all enough, exactly as we are.

# Six

# Body Talk

Something inside me has shifted since becoming a mum and I really believe pregnancy helped change my mindset on a lot of things.

Over the years I've been very overweight, worryingly thin and everything else in between, but regardless of my size, I have never felt attractive. The insecurities I have about my body have been with me my whole life and I doubt now that I'll ever get to a point where I can look at myself in the mirror and say I'm completely happy with how I look.

Those feelings are too deep-rooted.

But do you know what? Pregnancy and childbirth have definitely made me think: 'I might not love my body but look at what my body just managed!'

I might not always like what I see, but when my body faced its toughest challenge in my life so far, it didn't let me down and it did exactly what it was designed to do. I've got to be grateful and thankful for that. Yes, I've got a bit more meat on my hips than I'm used to these days but that means I can hold Ronnie there quite comfortably! And Jamie likes it too, so say no more . . .

That's what I'm going to try and hold on to, and body confidence is something I'm working really hard on. But when you've been as overweight as I have – at twenty-one I weighed over seventeen stone – it's almost impossible ever to see yourself as anything other than a 'big girl'.

You don't lose eight stone and then forget about it forever. The psychological scars from years of having low self-esteem, being laughed at, rejected and feeling unhappy with yourself don't seem to ever go away. At least they haven't for me.

I have been approached with offers to launch clothing ranges but I've politely declined; not because I didn't love the clothes but because you often have to model the collection personally with these things and I'm not able to put myself out there like that right now. I just can't.

After the cover shoot I did for *You* magazine, they gave me the photos but I couldn't bring myself to look at them. I had the best of the best make-up artists, hair stylists and photographer that day all working to make me look coverstar-ready, but I see things other people don't, and because of that, I find it difficult to look at myself.

While I've felt like this since as early as I can remember, these insecurities have definitely got worse over the last couple of years and that is magnified because my life and my job now involves being on screen with millions of people watching my stories. Eek!

I know I tell other people all the time to be happy and love themselves and 'you do you', but I find that harder when it comes to myself. I really wish I could just practise what I preach.

But I'm getting there.

Honestly, the encouragement, the support and the friendship I get from you guys inspires me every day – all of you are helping me accept myself for who I am and giving me the courage and confidence I've spent a lifetime looking for. And I really do love you for it.

My issues around my weight didn't really start until my late teens. I left school and it started to creep up without me even noticing really, especially after I passed my driving test and could drive myself to McDonald's and KFC. Oh dear. That's where all the trouble began!

My dad had bought me a black Renault Clio with quite a few years on the clock, and I loved that car. I remember buying my first little air freshener to go in it and thinking I was a proper grown-up driving around in my own set of wheels.

I actually managed to write it off one evening going round a bend where there had been an oil spill which skidded the wheels, and the car ended up in a ditch. It wasn't my fault, but it was the first accident I'd ever been involved in and it was one hell of a shock. And even though I was fine physically, the car was a complete goner.

After finishing sixth form and getting the telesales job in Chelmsford, I was earning my own money and using it to buy an awful lot of takeaways. I stacked on the pounds, and although I was twenty-one and should have been enjoying being young and free, instead I remember feeling miserable.

I wish I could have been one of those people who are comfortable in their own skin, no matter what their shape, but I've never been able to manage it. I think a lot of people who have been bigger will agree that you can often feel instantly judged because of your size. From overweight to underweight, I've experienced the full spectrum of attitudes and it's amazing how a lot of people treat you according to a number on a clothes label.

They look at you differently. When I was bigger, the way people looked at me, sometimes with what felt like disgust, made me feel dreadful. I'll never forget those looks. People make assumptions about you. You are automatically dismissed and ignored and you and your opinion become irrelevant. I just don't understand treating people in that way.

I'd get whispered about and overhear nasty comments and I hated going out to pubs and bars and seeing those looks which seemed to say: 'What is the likes of you even doing out the house?'

I'd be talked down to by men who thought if they gave

me any attention at all they were doing me a favour I should be eternally grateful for. I was desperately unhappy and found every day a struggle. My size made me feel like I didn't belong anywhere and that I was taking up too much room and always getting in someone's way.

Of course I tried loads of different diets and joined Slimming World when I was nineteen. I stepped on to the scales at my first meeting and saw '17 stone 4 pounds' staring back at me. That was a real shock for me.

'Woah,' I thought. I had no idea that I'd got that heavy.

I was easily one of the heaviest people there but I really wanted to do something about it and I stuck to every letter of the plan. I lost nine pounds in my first week and felt on top of the world.

I went on my own to the meetings, which you'll probably know by now was a big deal for me. I'd get weighed, buy my little Hifi bars and all my bits for the week ahead and I really got into it. The weight came off pretty steadily – I managed to lose two and a half stone over the next few months – and I started to feel better about myself.

My mum would say: 'Well done, Soph, you're looking really well!'

I felt like it, too.

But then along came a week where I gained a couple of pounds, which happens to most members at some point. The best response to that is to accept it, put it behind you, get straight back on the horse and return the next week with a loss.

I didn't do that.

Instead, I got disheartened and stopped going to the meetings. It made me feel embarrassed and I couldn't face going back. And over the next few weeks and months, I put all the weight I'd lost back on again, plus a bit more.

After that I was too ashamed ever to go back. I should have carried on, I know. I wish I had.

I wrote about the most humiliating moment of my life so far in *Hinch Yourself Happy*, but it's important to come back to it here because it totally was the straw that broke the camel's back. It happened at Peter Pan's theme park in Southend (it's called Adventure Island now but it'll always be Peter Pan's to me!) and I was so big that I couldn't fit on the ride. The safety bar wouldn't come down and I had to get off, feeling like the whole world was watching, pointing and laughing.

That was it. I knew I had to do whatever it took, however drastic. I wasn't enjoying my life. I wasn't 'living' at all, really. Never mind fairground rides, I couldn't fit comfortably in the back of a cab to go out with the girls. All of my clothes felt tent-like or had elasticated waists – I couldn't even find shoes to fit properly. I realise now with hindsight that I just didn't know how to dress properly for my size, because I see so many bigger girls who look absolutely incredible these days. That just wasn't me.

Those of you who have read my first book will know

what happened next, but I didn't want to dwell too much on it then as it still felt quite raw. It's only now that I feel ready to completely open up about what I went through.

After that horrendous experience at Peter Pan's I came home and googled 'best way to lose weight' and the first thing that popped up on the search results was a gastric band. I did a bit of reading up ('a bit' suggesting not nearly enough) and that was me, I was sold. This, so I thought, was going to solve all of my problems.

I phoned up a clinic and within a fortnight I'd taken out a £6,000 loan from the bank (I know, I know!) and was getting the band fitted. It's a huge amount of money and on my salary it was going to take me flipping years to pay off, but that's where my head was at. I was willing to put myself into massive debt for the chance to feel 'normal'. For the chance to feel happy. I really did think it was the only option I had left.

I kept it all to myself and didn't tell any of my friends or even my mum. I knew I'd get talked out of it when my mind was already set, and Mum would have been so upset I couldn't bear to think about it.

She'd also have given me a right old ear-bashing, so it was easier to say nothing and crack on and get it sorted.

The only person who knew was Trace because we worked together and I had booked a week off to have the operation.

'You're bonkers, Soph,' she said, shaking her head when I told her.

It was hard to disagree with her, to be fair.

I actually can't believe that I didn't worry more, but you know me: dive straight in and think about the what ifs later. If I'd known what problems this band would cause me in the future, I would never have done it. The words 'gastric band' literally give me the shivers now.

But on the other hand, I can see that I needed it. I saw it as the last resort and to this day I'm convinced I wouldn't have lost the weight on my own because I have no bloody willpower when it comes to food. I use it as a coping mechanism – I'm a big comfort eater and a lot of my bad habits relate to how I'm feeling at that particular time.

So without doing something extreme like getting the band, I think I would have continued to pile on the pounds, become more and more depressed about it and I honestly don't know where that would have left me.

I was put under general anaesthetic for the operation but was out of hospital the same day. It all seemed so straightforward. They put a silicone band around the upper part of my stomach, reducing it in size, which limited the amount of food I could eat. There's a tube attached to the band which they can access through a port sewn under the breastbone – the surgeon uses this port to inject saline solution into the band to inflate it, and this can be used to adjust the level of how much it tightens around the tummy, reducing the amount of food you're able to hold in your stomach. That's how it works, and obviously the fewer calories you are able to eat, the more weight you'll lose.

The morning after I'd had it done, I was in my flat and I nearly fainted from the pain coming from the port – I had painkillers but I'm terrible for remembering to take things like that and so I was in agony.

But after that initial shock, it seemed OK. It was all done by keyhole surgery so there was no scarring; it was just a case of me getting used to my new way of eating.

For the first few days, diet is restricted to just liquids before you work your way up to blended foods. Then you can introduce soft foods before you start experimenting with solids again, but it takes a lot less food to end up feeling full.

I tried to eat but would throw it back up or be in a lot of pain with what felt like really bad indigestion for hours on end. I didn't want to feel that pain so that made me too nervous to eat. I think there's an idea that the pounds simply fall off you after a gastric band but in fact, the weight loss is very slow at first. It's definitely not a quick fix, although you're left with no choice but to have a very different way of life.

And it involves a hell of a lot of soup! Soup, soup and more soup.

The fact that the weight was coming off little by little meant that people didn't really notice or comment on the fact I was getting thinner, so I didn't ever really need to explain myself. I wasn't going to be able to keep it a secret forever, though.

One evening, a couple of months after the surgery, I

went for a McDonald's drive-thru with the girls and, still not wanting to tell them what I'd done, I played it cool and ordered a Big Mac and fries.

I thought maybe, just maybe, it would be OK.

Er, how wrong was I? After a few bites of the burger, the pain was so dreadful that it made me double over, grabbing my stomach, and I had to come clean. I held my hands up and told them that I hadn't been hiding it from them on purpose; it just had never felt like the right time. The longer time went on, the harder it had felt to mention it.

They were all massively supportive (although they told me I'd officially lost the plot!) and I wished I had told them sooner. I still didn't dare tell my mum and dad, though.

The weight carried on dropping off and by the following year in 2012 when I started working at the recruitment agency and met Jamie, I was down to about 12 stone.

Unfortunately, though, this is me we're talking about and so obviously it was never going to be that simple. Sure enough, in 2013, the band slipped and it ended up wedged in my oesophagus. If you think that sounds horrendous, you are absolutely bloody right.

They say slippage happens to one in 4,000 bandsters (as we're apparently known – a name I hate, by the way!) and yes, I was warned of the risks beforehand, but you never think it's going to happen to you, do you? And you practically sign your life away when you go private so there was no possible comeback.

I'd been having terrible cramps which should have been a red flag that something was up, but I'd ignored them and hoped a load of Gaviscon would do the trick. I was pretty much living off that to get rid of the pain.

The day it all came to a head, I was with my mum, who of course still didn't know about the band. I started bringing up what looked like coffee granules. I screamed because it felt like my throat was on fire from all the acid coming up and burning my oesophagus.

I was swallowing whole ice cubes, trying to stop the burning, but they couldn't get past the band and were coming straight back up covered in blood.

'What's going on?' my mum cried, desperation in her voice, and she bundled me into the car and took me to hospital where I passed out in the waiting room.

Obviously I had no choice but to tell her then. I'd kept this huge secret from her for two years and she was heartbroken, as I knew she would be.

'Why are you doing this to yourself, Soph? Please, I'm begging you, leave yourself alone.'

'I'm so sorry, Mum,' I said tearfully. 'I just didn't know what else to do.'

After I was seen by the doctors, who confirmed that the band had slipped and I would need surgery immediately to fix it, she rang my dad.

'You've got to come down the hospital. It's Sophie, she's got to have an operation on her stomach. Just come to the hospital and I'll explain everything then.'

I had emergency surgery to move the band back to my stomach, but they left it unclipped so it wasn't so restrictive on how much food I could manage. I remember coming round from the anaesthetic and hearing my dad's voice.

'It's OK, it's OK,' he said, softly. 'Papa bear is here.'

It was lovely hearing that familiar voice but at the same time I didn't want to wake up and get a telling off, so I pretended to still be under the anaesthetic for a while! I heard my mum saying to the doctor: 'Can you take that *alien* out of her stomach now?'

And the doctor told her he was sorry but I was over eighteen so that decision was up to me.

I had some time off work to recover but didn't tell anyone the real reason. Me and Jamie were still just mates at the time but he'd noticed I'd been off sick and he would text to make sure I was OK. That made me like him even more; he was so caring and genuine.

Obviously he never knew me when I was my biggest and I certainly never told him about my past. He once saw a picture of me taken when I was bigger and asked who it was and I couldn't bring myself to tell him.

When I'd say I didn't like the way I looked, at first he thought I was deliberately fishing for compliments. He saw me completely differently to how I saw myself and so thought surely I couldn't really believe the things I was saying. It wasn't until we'd been together for a few months that he really understood it.

'You really don't see this, do you?' he said. 'You're so beautiful but you can't see it yourself.'

And that's when I told him everything about the gastric band and how I used to look. It felt like a huge relief to have it out in the open and he couldn't have been more lovely about it. He didn't judge me or criticise me or express any horror at what I'd done. He listened and tried to understand and told me he was proud of me and that he would still think I was beautiful whatever my size. He still says that now and I do believe him.

Sadly, though, there were even worse complications to come. The weight loss left me with excess skin on my arms so I went to see a surgeon to discuss having it removed.

I was all out of proportion and I mentioned in *Hinch Yourself Happy* that the extra skin was catching on fabrics, causing blisters and constantly bleeding. Some of the older blisters were even starting to scar.

It was summer and I couldn't get my arms out. I'd lost the weight but I was still having to cover up. He was an amazing surgeon and he said the state of my arms was so severe that I qualified to have the operation to remove the excess skin on the NHS.

They said before the surgery that there was a risk of infection and I did my usual: 'yeah, yeah, yeah, that won't happen to me' routine.

And obviously it did. Surprise, surprise.

The surgery itself went well but in the days after the op I started to get fluey symptoms and my arms blew up in size. I returned to hospital and the surgeon realised that I had an internal infection in my left arm and that both of them needed to be drained urgently. That's when I finally thought: 'OK, Soph. You've gone too far now.'

I ended up having to stay in hospital for two weeks and for a short, unbelievably scary time, there was a very real fear that I might lose my left arm. I was put on a course of IV antibiotics that killed the infection, thank God, and I had to sit up in bed with my arms hooked through these giant hoops so they could drain. What a mess. All because of this bloody band!

My poor body. It's gone through such a lot and I know I'm my own worst enemy. Because then of course came the complications I spoke about earlier on in this book during my pregnancy with Ronnie, which meant I had to have an operation under general anaesthetic to move the band when it was causing another blockage. Even though it was unclipped and inactive by that stage, it had been pushed upwards by me having a baby in my belly and I was unknowingly limiting my calorie intake and losing weight at exactly the time I needed to be putting it on.

As soon as I came out of hospital after the surgery and could eat properly again, I gained weight very quickly. My pregnant body had been starved for so long and therefore clung very gratefully on to every calorie I gave it.

Ronnie was born seven weeks later and I carried on putting on weight after his birth, gaining a further stone and a half in the first few months he was here.

I hated my body all over again. It felt like I was seeing the old me, the pre-gastric band Sophie, and the thought of ever going back to those days when I was bigger petrifies me. My mum is convinced that I've got body dysmorphia, which is a mental health condition where you obsessively worry about the 'flaws' you think you see in your physical appearance. She has said for a long time that I should get support for it, and my mum is very rarely wrong when it comes to anything that involves me, so maybe I need to take that on board.

And you know, the funny thing is, even when I was at my thinnest I wasn't happy with my body then either! Body shaming works both ways, and I got plenty of agg online when I was underweight, too.

I remember having this little bone which stuck out from my shoulder and I would get paranoid about that, not wanting anyone to notice it and think I was too thin.

When I was big, all I wanted was to be slim and thought that was what I needed to feel good about myself. But it clearly wasn't, and I realise now that these issues are way more complicated than just what I weigh.

With me, there's a twofold issue when it comes to body consciousness, because there's also my height to consider, which means that even when I've been at my thinnest, I still felt manly and masculine.

I'm 5 foot 10 inches and people have always commented on it. I've had: 'You're a big girl' and 'Wow, aren't you tall!' all my life.

I know they might mean it as a compliment, but to me it feels the same as saying, 'Oh my God, you're really over-weight!', which obviously most people wouldn't dream of saying.

I was around thirteen when I had some sort of growth spurt and suddenly shot up. I remember seeing a photo of myself standing next to the Christmas tree and I was practically the same height. It shocked me and was the first time I was really aware of my size, and I hated it.

All the other girls at school seemed to be feminine and petite while I just kept on growing. They'd be having fun experimenting with fashion whereas I used to dread being invited to a party because if I put on a pair of heels, I looked like a giant compared to everyone else.

My heart would sink as the girls discussed what they'd be wearing to go out that evening and I'd sit there think-ing: 'Oh no, it's one of these "heels" events.'

You know those flat shoes older ladies wear with the big bit of Velcro across the bridge of the foot? I confided in my mum once that I couldn't wait to be old so no one my age would be wearing heels any more and we'd all be in those types of flat shoes.

At that moment, I would have given anything to click my fingers and go straight to being a pensioner just for it all to go away. How mad is that! At first Mum laughed at me (and I know it sounds like a crazy thing to say), but after a couple of minutes she got a bit upset.

'Soph, it's really sad that you would happily wish away

that amount of time to be at an age where you no longer feel left out.'

Mum's right; it *was* sad. But I've always wanted to be a ladylike, petite, feminine kind of girl who can wear heels and not stand out in a crowd. I want to be able to stand up in a group and not be the one towering over everyone else. I find myself hunching my shoulders and crouching down in every picture I pose for with my Hinchers, trying to shrink myself to a more acceptable size.

I've tried to love – or, at the very least, accept – my height because I know there's nothing I can do about it – it's not like you can have your knees shaved down, because believe me, I've looked into that!

I see other tall girls carrying their height with such grace and confidence and I'd give anything to walk proud like that, but it's still the one thing I would change tomorrow if I could. I'm thirty now and I struggle with it more than ever.

Mum tries to build me up and points out that catwalk models are tall and that people would kill for my long legs. She tells me my height is a gift. The way I'm trying to look at it is how it might be able to benefit Ronnie. Me and Jamie are both tall and the signs are there that Ronnie will be too. So maybe we're going to have a little boy who will inherit our height and work that to his advantage. He could use it to be a basketball player or to be a goalie for Arsenal if he wanted to.

Oh my God, Jamie would so love that! So maybe

Mum's got a point and my height is going to be a gift in that way.

I'd love to have a little girl one day, and I know that if I do she may very well get my height. I hope she'll be able to embrace it in a way I've so far not been able to. At least she would have me to relate to – there were no tall women in my family when I was growing up and so I had no one who looked like me, which I think made it even harder. I felt like the odd one out. My dad's mum was tall, but sadly, I never got to meet her.

I do worry about passing on my insecurities to my children. It's something I'm very aware of and I'm determined not to let it happen. I will never put myself down in front of Ronnie or any other little ones we go on to have, and I will make it my life's mission to build them up and make them proud of who they are.

I'm also trying to take a little bit of control back with my own situation, and just before Christmas last year, I started on a diet. Nothing extreme, just sensible eating to lose the weight I'd gained after pregnancy slowly and steadily. My BMI is now where it should be and I'd say I'm in an OK place with my body at the moment. I'm hoping that this will be a good starting point to work on the deeper underlying issues, and also some of my other vulnerabilities.

I don't want to be skinny, but losing weight can be addictive, and so I know I've got to tread very carefully. I also know I look happier when I'm a healthy weight, and Jamie prefers me to have curves and a bit of something to hold on to!

He tells me: 'Babe, you're a woman, a mum, and that's the most attractive thing in the world!'

I do feel good when he says that.

I really want to be a responsible influencer and promote a healthy body image. Maybe one day I can find the balance between being a good role model and keeping my own negative body image in check. Or even stop battling it altogether and accept myself for who I am. No one is you, and that is your power.

I also hope that by telling my story I've helped some of you guys. When I put my ten-year 'transformation' picture up on Instagram last year, it was the hardest post I've ever done. I could have thrown up, revealing my past as a bigger girl to the world and not knowing how it was going to be received. But I felt like I had to do it, otherwise the weight loss story might have somehow come out in the press anyway.

I wrote a little note alongside the 'then and now' pictures.

'Whatever perception you may have of how perfect someone's life may appear,' I wrote, 'we never really know what people are going through inside. Please never judge a book by its cover and always be kind.'

The feedback and the replies were out of this world,

with thousands upon thousands of you saying: 'We love you even more now, Mrs Hinch!'

Jamie told me he was so proud of me because I'd spent the past decade trying to cover up who I was, and the wave of positivity that post resulted in far outweighed any of the nasty comments (naturally there were a few of them – #blocked). People were saying it had completely changed the way they thought of me because they had assumed I was someone who had it all and everything had always landed in my lap.

Guys, trust me, I haven't. I've been there and I know what it's like to feel so low about yourself. I always say I'm a work in progress. I'm my own biggest critic and I know I could and should be kinder to myself. We talk so much about showing kindness to others and often forget about ourselves, don't we?

So I'm learning to accept compliments. Even when they come from Jamie, I get really shy and awkward. Isn't that crazy? My big issue is that I forget the compliments I receive and end up focusing on the nasty comments instead, and that's something I know I need to flip, which is much easier said than done.

So when someone says something nice about my hair or what I'm wearing, I'm trying my best to smile and say 'thank you very much' rather than blush, pull a face, wave it away and put myself down.

It's a very hard habit to break when you're so used to rejecting compliments, but it *is* lovely to be paid one and to have someone take the time to tell us something nice, and we should recognise that. I actually screenshot them a lot of the time and save them in a folder on my phone so that I have them to look back at on those days when I'm not feeling so great.

Starting my new skincare regime this year has also helped. Not only have I seen an improvement in my complexion which has given my confidence a little boost, but spending those extra few minutes on self-care each day has felt really positive. Give it a go if you don't already!

We all have such busy, fast-paced lives these days – we're always contactable and constantly connected to the rest of the world – so taking some daily 'me time' is much needed. Don't ever feel guilty for it, you deserve it.

And if I keep up the new routine, I swear it's going to knock years off me! People ask me all the time how I feel about cosmetic surgery, and I think there are pros and cons to it and everyone is entitled to do what will make them happy as long as it's done properly and they've been well informed and counselled beforehand.

It's certainly not a priority for me at the moment – I'd like another baby and it's not like I'm an underwear model! Also, you've seen that my luck with surgery has been thin on the ground so maybe it's best avoided.

I've got stretch marks, I've got scars on my arms from my operations, my body is so far from 'perfect' and isn't 'bikini ready', whatever that means, and it never will be. The very thought of being papped on holiday, where the sunshine means I may possibly have to get a limb out, strikes the fear of God into me. Actually, I heard someone say once that a 'bikini body' is just your own body (whatever it may be like) with a bikini on it, and I don't know why, but I love that. It made me smile. There's so much unnecessary pressure these days to look a certain way, and I think we all forget, me included, that having a healthy, functioning body should be the most important goal in all of this, and that's what we should be aiming towards.

Hearing all your stories about the personal challenges you've overcome is so inspiring to me. It reminds me that I'm not alone in this – we can all build each other up, and isn't that fantastic?

I'm not suggesting for one second that anyone go to the extremes I did to lose weight, quite the opposite actually. If sharing my experience makes anyone think twice before taking such drastic measures, then I think that's a good thing.

I'd like to look on my new decade as a chance to start again with the way I see myself. A reset button. As I head into my thirties, I want to try and stop beating myself up over my body. I wasted so much energy doing precisely that in my twenties and I really want the next chapter of my life to be different. I want to give myself a break. That's why I'm focusing so much on things like mindfulness, and how I speak to myself, and I make time to do those types of activities which I included in my *Activity*

*Journal*, because I find that they really help and it's so important to be kind to yourself.

So I'm going to focus on what my body has achieved rather than obsessing over what I want to change about it and hating myself if I gain a couple of pounds. Or feeling guilty for having a chocolate biscuit. Or stopping myself from having a dessert because I'm worried about fitting into my jeans.

I know now that there is more to life, and that's because of Ronnie.

Since walking out of the hospital having given birth, I look at every single woman differently. We are all absolute queens, with our strength and the extraordinary things that our bodies are capable of. We really are incredible.

It's why I can't understand why mums pull each other apart – we should be standing there saying: 'We are bloody women! We are so strong! Look at what we manage to do!'

For nine months, I grew a baby. I went through labour to bring him into the world and then I nourished him with my milk.

That's what my body did.

My body *is* perfect because it made Ronnie, and he is nothing short of a miracle.

# Seven

# The Truth About the Trolls

There are so many things about my life as Mrs Hinch that are nothing short of amazing. And I'm trying my very best, as much as I can, to focus my energy on those things. But there has also been a dark and completely devastating side to becoming 'Insta-famous' which you don't very often see me talk about.

And, to be honest, the true impact of it is something I'm not massively comfortable about sharing.

I've never wanted the people who have hurt me so badly and caused me so many tears, stress and sleepless nights, to know just how deeply they've affected me and my family. I've never wanted to give them that satisfaction because I know their minds are so warped that they would probably feel like they'd won. I'm at the stage where I feel like my unhappiness would be like some sort of victory to them.

It would be wrong of me to pretend that everything is always perfect, because it's definitely not, and the trolling from a small but relentless group of haters who, it seems, are set on taking me down, has been so horrific at times that I have decided it's time for me to finally speak out and share with you the sorts of things I have been going through.

So, deep breath, Soph. Here goes.

The truth is, away from my life that you see on Instagram, these people have almost destroyed me, and the fact that I am on medication for depression and anxiety for the first time in my life is largely down to what they have put me through.

As I said earlier on, I'm not ashamed to admit that I'm on antidepressants. I don't think anyone should ever feel embarrassed to admit that they need help. But I'm so sad that this is what it's come to.

I know I'm being watched by lots of people who love me (and who I love right back!) and that 98 per cent of those who follow me I am blessed to have in my life. But there are also others who make fun of me, pick apart everything I do, analyse every move I make and pull me apart for the things I say, for my appearance and for the way I speak.

These people flood my inbox with the most vile abuse. They direct-message me purely to attack me. They make cruel comments about my looks, they say my house is disgusting and they try and get me in trouble with industry regulators through egging each other on to report any of my posts where they think I've broken the rules, when I haven't. I will honestly never understand how they have the time to dedicate so much energy towards me. Can you imagine what they could be achieving if they redirected that energy and used it to do something positive in their own lives?

I understand now that I will never be able to do anything right in their eyes. For the longest time I have been trying to make sense and rationalise the thoughts and actions of irrational and unreasonable people. While I am making a real effort to try and take a different approach mentally with how I react to these things, the constant bullying has become so brutal in the past that it has triggered panic attacks, which I've managed to keep at bay for years, and they have left me bedridden.

It started slowly with one or two mean comments on my grid posts, and yes, they stung a bit, but they were easy enough to ignore. I'm not daft enough to think everyone's going to like me and I know with social media you sometimes have to take the rough with the smooth. But it wasn't like I was saying or doing anything offensive, so I never had any reason to think I would attract any real nastiness. I clean my house!

As my Instagram took off, the trolling steadily became worse, and what started as a few stupid comments that I was able to bat away quickly became something more sinister, and it now feels like a hate campaign against me – a daily rush of direct messages and nasty comments on my photos – with apparently absolutely nothing I can do about it. Which is just madness to me.

I have no comeback. I have no interest in getting involved in an online spat with anyone. I don't have the headspace for the stress it would cause me, so the only option I have is to delete the comments from my posts and block the people who DM me the hate.

But these individuals are so persistent that they just set up new accounts and come straight back. Again and again and again. It's like a weird game to them, as if they get some sort of thrill from it, but it's constant and exhausting for me and has tested my sanity at times.

It used to just be me logged into my Instagram account. You know how important that's always been to me. And if you ever get a DM or a comment from me, that of course will always be me personally and no one else. That will never change. But the horrible DMs I was getting were so bad and happening so often that someone on my team, one of my best friends, actually, saw how upset they were making me and stepped in. So she now keeps an eye on my inbox and grid posts for me and deletes and blocks as necessary. Nasty messages do still slip through the net, of course, because of the volume of DMs there are to go through, but things have been so much better since we've had this little system in place.

Unfortunately, it's not just on Instagram that I have to deal with people saying awful things about me. Comments underneath online newspaper and magazine articles not only tear me to shreds but have also shared private information about my family, and I have had to hire lawyers and publicists to fight those particular cases to get those things removed because it's actually illegal to disclose such information about people who aren't in the spotlight. I understand that because I have chosen to live my life in the public eye, I need to respect that people are allowed to have their say when it comes to me. But my family haven't chosen this life. How can it be right that people are allowed to do this?

So much of what I post ends up in the papers, and I'm going to be honest, half the time I don't understand it, because I don't get how us just living our lives can be considered news. Whether it's the latest Mrs Hinch hack or what me, Jamie and Ronnie have been up to, and even if the article itself is a really lovely one, the comments section gives these people who have a problem with me just another opportunity to be unkind.

By far the worst of the abuse takes place on online forums where groups of women, many of them mothers themselves – and I have no doubt some men – spend their spare time taking chunks out of me.

There is one particular site which is the worst. I'm not going to name it because it doesn't deserve the air time, but I do need to confront this head on as I think that running scared of them is what makes them assume they hold some power over me.

A lot of you will know about the site anyway, because it's quite notorious, and if you've ever made your way on there, you will know that it's an awful place. I'm convinced it exists only to ridicule, torment and abuse.

I'm one of many Instagrammers and social media people they target, and I know there are horrible conversations happening about lots of others who feel just as bullied as I do. But for some reason, I'm definitely Public Enemy Number One, with more posts and comments dedicated to me and everything I do than anyone else. I just don't understand it – it's like an obsession.

They question my abilities as a mother, pull to pieces everything I say, call me horrendous names and constantly report me to the ASA and the brands I work with before bragging about it to each other on the site. They send me abusive DMs on Instagram and then they'll post the screenshot on their website where their online friends will laugh and congratulate them. And the lies they spin about me – those are actually crazy. Laughable at this stage. They come up with conspiracy theories about me and my past, and why I do the things I do, that are actually insane. And it's almost like they've convinced themselves that their lies are the truth. I'm not sorry to say it, guys, but I'm just not that interesting. What you see with me is what you get. It's actually targeted harassment on the most unbelievable scale and it's affected me more than they could ever know.

I used to go on there to keep an eye on what they were saying, but it got way too much for me, and for the sake of my mental health, I have to make myself stay away now. It was becoming like an act of self-harm scrolling through post after post of hatred. I just can't put myself through that any more.

Even though I try my absolute best to avoid it now, a lot of my Hinchers monitor it and they will send me screenshots of what's being said, which I know is only out of love and concern for me but it also means I sometimes can't escape it if it's one of those messages that slip through the net.

Blatant lies about me, abuse and attacks every single day. It's brought back all of those nervous feelings from school, but this time it's so much worse. I didn't expect to be a grown woman in my thirties and still have to deal with this sort of stuff.

A particularly low point for me was when I posted my transformation photo in January 2019. Everyone on Instagram was doing the #10yearchallenge pic and it seemed like a fun thing to take part in, but it took me a lot of time and thought before I felt brave enough to join in. It was a really big deal for me.

Obviously I look very different to how I did ten years earlier, as it was before I had the gastric band put in and I was eight stone heavier. I knew that opening up about my past would give my followers a better understanding of who I was, where I'd come from and what I had gone through, but I was also worried the trolls would have a field day.

Finally, I found the courage. It was all going to come out eventually anyway, so I wanted to 'own it', as they say.

I pressed send and then I hid myself away, terrified about the reaction and too scared to look at my phone which immediately started to ping with notifications.

When I managed to bring myself to look, most of the responses were incredibly supportive and lovely and I'm so pleased that so many of you were touched by and could relate to my story.

But as I predicted, the trolls pretty much went into meltdown, the main accusation being that I was a liar and that the before picture wasn't really me and that I'd faked my own ten-year challenge. I mean, what the . . .

Why would I even do that? When you lose a large amount of weight, it does dramatically change your face, so obviously I'm going to look a bit like a different person. And even when they started to accept that OK, maybe it *was* me after all, they said in that case I must have had extensive cosmetic surgery on my nose, forehead and chin, which is completely untrue.

Just a few months later I was seriously ill in hospital having the operation to move the gastric band which, although unclipped, had caused a lot of issues. As I wrote earlier, during my pregnancy, the band had caused a blockage and was stopping food going into my stomach – I was extremely underweight even though I was only two months away from my due date.

The same people who were mocking my 'before' picture and who had nicknamed me Fat Soph (that's one of the kinder names I've been called) were now saying I was skinny and revolting and that I looked 'dead'.

'Imagine holding her, I'm surprised Jamie even touches her,' one of them wrote.

Another said: 'I couldn't bear to touch her horrible hands if she was the last person on the planet. Her face is disgusting.'

I'll remember those comments for as long as I live. I'm just so happy I only saw them once I'd come out of the hospital and was feeling a bit stronger, and not while I was in, terrified for the safety of my Ronnie and trying to focus on my recovery.

My hands oddly seem to be a popular topic of discussion. I'm my own worst enemy and yet they've made me paranoid about things I've never even noticed about myself before. Apparently my hands are 'disgusting, veiny and bony', but I have a medical condition which I'm on blood thinners for. I've got stents in to keep my blood flowing – it's not something I can help.

They slag off my nails for being unmanicured at times and say I'm filthy because I've not had them done in a while, but I have a baby to look after now and so manicures come very low down on the list of priorities these days.

I've actually become so paranoid about my hands that sometimes I wear rubber gloves when I don't even need to just so they don't have the ammunition. Or I try and warm up my hands to get rid of the veins before I do my stories.

I've tried (and I won't give up trying) to grow a thicker skin regarding the abuse directed at me, but when it's aimed at Ronnie I won't ever accept it. The fact that not even my baby is safe from their hate makes me seriously question humanity and everything about this public life that I've somehow become tangled up in. Me being in the firing line is one thing, but commenting on my innocent child is an entirely different kettle of fish that I will never tolerate. They attack the way he looks, criticise his development and all sorts of other sick and twisted spiteful things that I can't even bring myself to repeat.

I'm actually in tears writing this because he's my beautiful, innocent little baby boy; my world. I will never, ever understand people picking on a tiny, defenceless baby.

Who even does that? How can they live with themselves? It's just so cruel. And a lot of them are mothers themselves so you would think they'd know better. It actually makes me feel very sorry for their children.

They started on Ronnie right from when he was first born and I posted a picture of his little hand on my grid. It's hard to believe that anyone could find something to be nasty about in a photo like that, but they did. There really are no words.

They laughed at the shape of his head – Ronnie was sat very low during my pregnancy and so when he was born his head wasn't perfectly round. To me he was always perfect but to the trolls it was something else to pick on.

They trolled him for how his hair grows. When it started to grow in, he had the thickest little tufts around the sides like a grandad and I love it. That's my boy and anyone who follows me will know I adore those tufts. I couldn't cope with the cuteness! We call him tufters!

But to them it was another excuse to knock him.

They drag me through the mud for so many of my parenting choices and say I'm being a crap mum for what I feed him. What business is it of anybody else's if he has an Ella's Kitchen pouch every now and again? He loves them and they're organic, and all mothers do things differently, and whatever works for you is absolutely fine as long as your baby is being properly taken care of.

I got told things like 'your baby should be moving more', 'your baby should have teeth by now' and here I was thinking: 'Oh dear God. I'm a first-time mum so I don't know what is and isn't right.' Whatever I would see, I would end up questioning myself, and it was making me sick with worry.

A few months ago I mentioned on my stories that some of the digs about Ronnie were getting to me. By that point I'd had months of this, I was having a bad day and I suppose I was reaching out, not knowing where else to turn.

You guys were all so amazing. You reassured me that what Ronnie was doing was perfectly fine, normal and, most importantly, what is right for him. Every baby is different. They don't all develop teeth or start crawling at the same time and we shouldn't compare them to one another.

Before I got your kind messages of support, I didn't realise it was affecting me as much as it was, but I broke down as I read them. I think it was pure relief more than anything. I had been worrying that he was behind and that it was my fault. But after reading through your love and support and reassurance, I felt better. I have the best followers. I've always been so proud of my boy.

Ronnie is healthy and he is so loved, and I'm just grateful he's here after what we went through during the pregnancy. But I also feel guilty that I've put him out there for people to see. But why shouldn't I be able to share my beautiful boy with everyone like other people do?

If I'm perfectly honest, I'm obsessed with him! It doesn't make sense to me that he wouldn't be part of my life on Instagram. I see and read the love he gets every single day from my followers and it blows me away. He doesn't even realise how loved he is! So I just want to say thank you to every single one of you who has taken the time to send me lovely messages about Ron. I appreciate every single one of them and when I do come across them, I screenshot and save them in a Ron folder on my phone. I can't wait to show them to him one day when he is old enough to understand all of this!

It's something I've thought long and hard about and yes, I could take Ronnie away from Instagram. Me and Jamie have spoken about it at length. But he is my life and I can't believe he's here and he's real – he is perfection in my eyes and I want to shout about him to the world. Me and Jamie have this amazing little man and I want to share that.

Also, most of my followers have fallen in love with him

because they've been with us through our whole journey, so why should they have to miss out?

It's the trolling of Ronnie that made me realise how much these people must hate me. The reason they lay into him isn't because they despise him, it's because he's a part of me. And I truly believe this is just another way for them to get at me. To kick me where they know it'll really hurt me – my baby. To be fair, not even handsomes Henry is spared! How anyone can look at my beautiful boys and have anything negative to say is truly beyond me.

I know not everyone is going to like me and I totally get that I'm not to some people's taste, and that is absolutely fine. But what have I done for them to dislike me *that* much? I'm not a murderer or a criminal.

They could just accept that I'm not for them and forget about me and move on. Why would they project such hate on to my child and my dog? Why would they not go and follow people who they *do* like and who inspire them and make them happy?

Maybe then they'd be happier individuals, because surely contented people don't do things like this?

I'll admit that reading the sickening comments about Ronnie has broken me in the past. There have been days when I've not felt able to leave the house. Some mornings I've barely been able to make it out of bed.

I've had nights where I'd replay the abuse I'd read that day over and over in my mind and I'd be terrified of what was coming the next day. The bit of confidence I'd found in the last few years since meeting Jamie had been stripped away.

Things came to a head just before Christmas last year when the latest string of abuse and body-shaming triggered the worst panic attack I've experienced yet.

It started off as a normal evening at home and I posted a story of me sat on the floor wrapping presents.

It was a side view and so maybe not the most flattering angle. But, you know, Ronnie was only four months old, I still had my mum tum and I had no bra on and it didn't register to me that I needed to be all perfect and sucking everything in to sit and wrap gifts on our living-room floor.

I uploaded the video and the trolls went to town on me. My followers sent me a load of screenshots of them pointing out my weight gain and making horrible jokes about 'Fat Soph' being back.

They were saying things like: 'I can't wait for her to go back to being big again, let's see how happy she is being who she is then' and they changed the words of that football song to: 'She's coming home, she's coming home, Fat Soph's coming home.'

That's what tipped me over the edge.

I could feel the panic starting and I just remember thinking 'oh no, oh no', because I knew what was coming and that there was nothing I could do about it. My panic attacks begin as a tingling at the bottom of my back that creeps up over my shoulders and into my chest.

I screamed for Jamie and he came running in thinking I'd hurt myself.

I was hysterical, struggling to breathe, dripping in sweat, and it honestly felt like I was dying.

There was this sharp pain of nerves in the middle of my chest and a huge knot in my stomach which ached, I felt sick and I wanted to strip off everything I was wearing because I was sweating so much. Everything was whizzing past at 1,000 miles an hour. I couldn't focus on anything.

I remember I had my Sellotape dispenser gadget on my hand and I was desperately trying to shake it off but it was stuck and wouldn't come loose and that was making me worse. I was frantic.

For about twenty minutes Jamie had to breathe and pace me through it and gradually I calmed down. But although the physical symptoms had slowed, it took me several days to properly recover.

I got upset and annoyed with myself that it had happened and now I live in fear that it's going to happen again. I don't want to experience that, ever. That one isolated incident might not seem like a big deal to some, and it might be hard to understand why it caused me to panic so severely, but for me, it was a build-up of months and months and months of reading awful things about myself.

It was after that attack that I finally admitted I needed help and I went to the GP who prescribed me the medication I'm on now, which is helping me keep things on more of an even keel.

It all makes me extremely paranoid about going out, wondering if I'm going to come across one of these people that dislike me so much. They know who I am and I know they are watching me, but I don't know who they are, and the thought of walking past one of them in the street is very unsettling.

I'm always wondering if people I pass could be one of the faceless bullies who have been vicious about my lovely baby or who hate me so much that they would cause me to become ill.

When I catch wind of someone saying my name, my first thought is one of dread that it might be one of them. Thankfully, it's never happened, and as far as I know, everyone who has ever stopped me in the street has been lovely.

I genuinely believe a lot of these trolls are in need of help. A Hincher once inboxed me with screenshots of posts from another Instagram user who clearly detested me. She had written loads of comments on Instagram posts saying I was vile, I was fake, she couldn't stand me and I was this and I was that and all the names under the sun. She'd posted pictures of my face zoomed in to make fun of the way I looked.

Just out of curiosity, I clicked on her profile and realised she was actually someone who had sent me loads of DMs.

But it wasn't to send me hate. To my surprise, they were all lovely, lovely messages.

It was all: 'Oh Mrs Hinch, you've changed my life, you're my inspiration, here's a picture of my handsomes, my baby boy is only two weeks younger than Ronnie, I couldn't wake up and not see your stories.'

And I thought: 'What is this world?'

I didn't contact her about it – what good could have come of that? – I just left it and blocked her. But I don't understand it. And I never will. How weird to be a follower and send me such wonderful messages while at the same time tearing me to shreds all over the internet. It's things like this that make me question their sanity.

Another time I was at the supermarket and the woman at the till next to me was £3 short for her shopping. She was just about to put some things back but I overheard what was going on and I offered to pay for the whole lot. She was so lovely and so grateful, and I never told anyone about it because that's not why I did it. To be honest, I forgot all about it and carried on with my day.

Two weeks later I saw a post on a Facebook group slagging me off to high heaven. God knows what I'd done to upset them that day. Breathed the wrong way, probably. One of the people posting on that horrible thread joined in with the hate and joked that: 'Haha, at least I got some free food out of her.'

'Surely not,' I thought to myself.

But I went on to her profile and saw her photo – it was

definitely the woman in the shop because I recognised the child in the picture.

That was a real kick in the teeth. I felt like a complete mug. I wished I'd spent that money on Ronnie instead of someone like her.

I don't know how websites that host these forums for people to troll are allowed to exist. It's modern-day bullying in open view, plain and simple. I have read it and not been able to eat and then cried myself to sleep. They are not the harmless gossip sites they're dressed up to be. They are dangerous and something needs to be done about them.

If these sites were taken off the internet tomorrow, I know that my life and the lives of so many others would change for the better and our mental health would be in a completely different place.

I don't understand who would choose to be part of a gang like that where you get praised for being the biggest bully. I'd rather be on my own like I was when I was younger, eating my packed lunch on the school steps. One thing that I've read so often, when I've gone down the rabbit hole about this particular site, is that they're allowing people their right to freedom of speech. While I'm all for freedom of speech, there is a way to get your point across in a constructive manner where you don't have to be rude, and also my Hinchers have told me time and time again that they've made accounts just to defend me, because they've been so upset by the things they've read, and their comments have either been deleted or they've been blocked off the site entirely.

We've spoken a lot about how important being kind is this year, but sadly it seems like people so quickly forget. The trolls didn't even have a day off when the country was in lockdown and everyone was dealing with personal heartaches, tragedies and fears about the future. They just carried on throughout.

Before this Instagram world I never understood why someone would take their own life. Even the word . . . I couldn't comprehend it.

But sadly, I understand now. This is not me saying it's something I've even considered, because I haven't. And please don't think that I'm saying I ever think it's the only solution, because I want people to know there is always, *always* another way. There is always help out there and you are so loved and you deserve to be here. You are never alone.

But I definitely get how someone can be pushed to the edge and feel like there is no way out because you just want all the noise to stop.

The tragic news about Caroline Flack's death broke when we were at Disneyland back in February. I didn't know Caroline personally but I have watched and loved her for years.

She was such a beautiful lady; funny, talented, so well-loved, and while it's not right to point fingers of blame because there was obviously a lot going on in her life

when she did what she did and these are always complicated stories, what she had been subjected to during her
years in the public eye must have taken its toll and been
unbearable at times.

It was actually a Hincher who told me the dreadful
news. I was in the queue for some food at the hotel restaurant and she came up to me and said: 'Soph, have you
heard that Caroline Flack has passed away?'

I was holding a plate of food which I suddenly lost all
my appetite for. I felt sick. I left the buffet queue and went
over to where my mum was sitting and told her.

Straightaway my mum was looking at it from the perspective of a mother with her daughter in the spotlight. I
could see it in her face. Her expression completely changed.
She was worried.

She sat me down that night back at the hotel and we
had such a deep conversation, just me and her.

She said: 'Soph, can you please promise me that if you
ever feel that all this is getting out of control, you will
tell me.'

She held me tight and added: 'I need to know you're
enjoying this and that you will tell me if you're not
OK.'

And I promised her that I would. I will never tell her
every detail of what I struggle with each day because I
don't want to worry her unnecessarily, but I will definitely
let her know if it ever gets too much.

Mum didn't let go of me that night, she just wanted to

keep me close, I think. When we went on our evening walk after dinner, she linked my arm the whole time, rubbing my hand and squeezing me tight. She even put me to bed and tucked me in, just like she used to when I was younger. As a kid, I could never sleep until she'd done that.

And when she said goodnight, it was more than just that word. I heard the love and the emotion in her voice and I knew it was her saying to me: 'We are here, you are safe, please never get to that place.'

I had so many inbox messages that night from my Hinchers, who were also so upset from the news and checking if I was OK. Even though I don't tend to discuss trolls on my stories, my followers are tuned in enough to know how these things affect me without me telling them. Sometimes it feels like you guys know me better than I know myself.

If I'm honest, Caroline's death has made me more scared. It was gut-wrenching and made me question everything.

There are only so many comments you can read over and over about the way you look, talk and act until you start to believe that it's true and you look at yourself in the mirror and you no longer see the person you thought you were.

The thought that Ronnie might go online one day and read all of this about his mum and about himself is incredibly painful. Hopefully, if he's anything like Jamie, it'll be meaningless to him and he'll be able to laugh it off.

Jamie has the skin of a rhino. He knows it's out there

but he couldn't care less and isn't even tempted to read it. He doesn't care about those trolls. They could say anything they like about him and he would just roll his eyes and get on with the rest of his day as if nothing had happened. In fact, he'd probably laugh.

Even when they say stuff about Ronnie, he's like, 'whatever, if you're making comments about a baby, you're not right in the head, see you later', and just forgets about it. I so wish I was like that. I wish I could be more like Jamie!

I've asked him why he doesn't get upset and he says to me: 'If anyone says my wife is ugly, look at her: she ain't. If anyone says my baby's not right, look at him: he's perfect. If anyone wants to take down the way I live my life, then whatever – I'm living my best life. Whatever they say is rubbish and none of it means a thing to me.'

Isn't that an amazing attitude to have? He gets frustrated for me and he hates seeing me torture myself over it, but he doesn't let their cruel words bother him in the slightest.

I've thought a hell of a lot about what can be done to tackle trolls when not even a tragedy like Caroline's is enough to stop them, because from what I've seen, the situation is worse than ever. There's certainly been no let-up from where I'm standing. How can we change this terrible culture of online harassment and nastiness? Why are people allowed to be part of online communities solely dedicated to bullying?

I don't have all the answers, but I do have some ideas which I think are worth looking into.

For a start, I don't think you should be allowed to be anonymous on these sites. If you're going to troll someone, grow some balls, stand by your words and your opinions and be a face. Show yourself. People shouldn't be allowed to be anonymous so that not even Instagram knows who they are. That makes no sense to me, because if it spills over into harassment and bullying then you should be able to be reported, traced and brought to justice. You should never treat someone online in a way you wouldn't treat them if you met them in the street.

I'd also really like to see mental health and the effects of online platforms and social media being discussed much more in schools.

It was good to hear that some schools have been showing students the award-winning *Odd One Out* documentary by Jesy Nelson from Little Mix, who tried to take her own life when the trolling became too much. It's difficult to watch, but the message is so important. When I saw the show, my heart broke for Jesy, but she's such a brave girl for speaking out.

Of course, it's not just influencers and celebs who get abused; kids need to see this, too.

These days, the bullying doesn't stop at the school gates. Kids carry on being taunted and teased at home online meaning there is no let-up from it. I have no idea how I would have coped if WhatsApp and Facebook had existed when I was at school and it's one of the reasons why I'm so passionate about my work with the children's charity Place2Be.

This is happening to ordinary people with serious bullying going on all around us. People have to understand that their words really do have consequences, whoever you are.

By going back to basics and starting to talk about this in the classroom, maybe we can stop the next generation growing up in such a toxic environment. I certainly don't want this to be Ronnie's world.

The platforms themselves should be doing so much more to combat the problem and show that they are taking it seriously. I know they've started. I wish they would get a handle on it, but nothing seems to be changing. Everything should be monitored more aggressively, trolls should be removed and prevented from coming back under a new account, and hateful comments should be immediately deleted because it's out of control and ruining people's lives.

To better understand it myself, I'd actually love to meet some of these people who detest me the most, sit down with them and really get to the bottom of why it is they do this. Really understand what it is they get out of it.

I'd ask them why I've upset them so much. I wouldn't want to attack them, I'd just want to know why. And I'd listen. Is there anything I could do to help? I'd really like to find out what is going on in their lives that is making them behave like this. What would it take for them to stop?

It's hard to imagine that people might just be nasty for the sake of it without needing any reason, but maybe that's just what I've got to accept. I'm sad that this is part of my life now to the extent that being abused has become a normal thing that I just have to learn to live with.

If I didn't have Jamie, my family and my friends and you guys – my amazing Hinchers who will always have my back – I honestly don't know what I'd do.

But I refuse to spend the rest of my life feeling like this.

My sister recently told me that when my Instagram first started getting bigger, she was worried for me. She knew how sensitive I was and she thought the attention – good and bad – was either going to make me or break me.

'It was going to go either way, Soph,' she said. 'And I was scared for you and all of us.'

Then she added: 'But despite what you might think, it's made you. You are more confident but you don't see it. It's made you stronger but you don't realise it, it's made your skin thicker but you can't feel it.'

She's right. I don't see it, but it was lovely to hear and I'm trying to convince myself what she's said is true, because then I feel like Superwoman! For a few minutes, at least.

I might feel like the trolls have broken me in the past, but I promise you, I'm piecing myself back together. I'm stronger now than I've ever been and I will fight this.

I won't be silenced, and they won't win.

I haven't told you all of this because I want anyone to feel sorry for me. Things have got so much better since I stopped torturing myself by reading every little thing I saw about myself online. I would seek things out, and I don't do that any more. Of course I still come across the odd DM or comment, or I'll stumble by an account set up to troll me because they like to use my hashtags to get my attention. But I remind myself that these must be desperately unhappy people if this is how they get their kicks. How they treat me says so much more about them and what's going on in their lives. I realise now that it's not about me, or anything I've done, not really. I'm an incredibly forgiving person and I genuinely hope that they find their peace one day.

I tell myself this is a really good journey I'm on and it's happened for a reason. I have such a beautiful life and so many exciting things to look forward to and no one can take any of that away from me.

# Eight
# Myths and Misconceptions

I have read plenty of conspiracy theories about me and my life since this whole journey began. These misconceptions aren't abusive or unkind, just completely daft, and some are so bizarre that the only option really is to laugh. There are so many weird and wonderful (and quite frankly, just completely wrong) speculations about me, Mrs Hinch and how all of this came about, and I probably hear a different one every week, each one more crazy than the last!

I understand that there are a lot of people who love a good conspiracy theory, even if most of them are a load of absolute rubbish. They do get people talking and thinking.

When I read things that come out about people in the public eye, I now take them with a pinch of salt because I realise, after my own experiences, they're only really guesswork and are often based on very little fact. That's the whole point, I guess. The truth is far more boring than what people can make up and assume.

Me and Jamie can't believe how ridiculous some of the stories we have heard are, and yes, at the beginning I did get quite upset by them. I'd be thinking: 'How can it be right that there are so many lies out there about me?' And some of the blatant crap that I read in the papers is just completely made up. It can be really hard sometimes desperately wanting to set the record straight, and not being able to. I'd want to go and shout them down from the rooftops and stop people spreading them round.

These days, I'm a lot more relaxed about them. I have more important things to focus my attention on and I find them more frustrating now than anything else.

I tend not to comment on them, but I thought now might be as good a time as any to address a few of the most insane and knock them all down.

Forget the dust-busting, let's do some myth-busting!

### 'The Mrs Hinch phenomenon was all manufactured by a management company.'

How hilarious! To this day I don't know how all of this happened and I never will. All I am, and all I continue to be, is grateful. If you asked me how to do it all again, I wouldn't even know where to start. I didn't have any sort of management until my Instagram was well established. I had several different management companies approach me, and I only decided I needed one when my account became bigger than I knew how to comfortably handle myself.

If this was all a set-up and planned, I wouldn't have bothered to go and get my hairdressing qualification six months before I started my account. That just doesn't make any sense to me.

It's not possible to cook up something as unpredictable and unusual as this, otherwise surely everyone would be doing it?

I didn't even know what an 'influencer' actually was. The management company I'm with represent some of the biggest influencers in the UK, and I know they won't mind me saying, but I had honestly never heard of any of them before I joined the same agency. This whole world is completely new to me. I had a personal Instagram account, of course, and I'd started my Mrs Hinch account when we bought our first house (@mrshinchhome_x_, as it was in those days) but I had no experience of anything near this sort of scale.

### 'She always wanted to be famous.'

I know I say this an awful lot, but I will never see myself as famous. And people thinking that I've always wanted to be 'famous' couldn't be further from the truth; the complete opposite actually. It's one of the main reasons I kept my face off my account for so long. For the longest time, you'd only ever see my hands, and that's the way I liked it. If I wanted to be famous, surely I would have plastered myself all over my account? It's the one thing about Instagram I'd change now if I had the choice; to not be recognised, because it makes me feel so anxious. I so wish I could carry on being part of this amazing Hinching community without being well known. It's another reason why you haven't seen me on the telly much. I've turned down loads of TV offers because I didn't want my face to become any more familiar than it already is.

### 'It's all Jamie's masterplan – he's the one pulling the strings.'

Oh gosh, I hear this one a lot and it is so sexist. It basically suggests a woman couldn't possibly generate success on her own – she would only be able to if there was a man controlling everything.

It really annoys me, actually. Why, as a woman, can't I have created this myself? I'm strong enough to grow a human and give birth and keep a roof over our heads. And I've done all of that without owning a pair of balls!

Jamie is very clued up on everything now because he's had to be, but when this all started, he had no idea what was going on either so the idea that he masterminded it all is quite funny.

He would come home from work and say: 'Babe, the girls in the office say you've got more followers and they're going up quick. What are you doing?'

And I'd say: 'Start watching my stories, then. See what you think.'

He says himself he is my number one fan for so many reasons and he watches me every single day, but there is no way on earth that he has in any way influenced me to do this. If anything, he's the one who tells me to give it up when he sees how anxious I get with it all.

## 'People are being hoodwinked because she's a professional saleswoman, not an Essex housewife.'

OK, so one day it's all Jamie's idea, another it's a cunning plot by a management agency and the next it's all down to me. Jeez, it's hard to keep up!

Years ago, I used to sell 0800 numbers to businesses. In fact, I've worked selling a mixture of things from telecoms to advertising, but that's no secret and I've never lied about my sales past. It's in my first book. If I wanted to hide the fact I have worked in sales before, why would I publish it for everyone to read? But it's not relevant to what I do now in the slightest.

If the conspiracy theorists think I'm some hotshot super saleswoman and have used my special manipulative powers to get everyone hooked, then they are massively overestimating my talents and skills. Maybe I should be flattered!

## 'She makes money from every product she shows on her account.'

Uhm, absolutely not! First of all, I was already showing most of the products I still talk about today on my account before I worked in partnership with any of those brands. So when I was approached by them to work in collaboration, of course I jumped at the chance. They are products that I have tried, tested and loved for years. I was so flattered to even be asked to work with some of my favourite companies. I've also had the amazing opportunity as part of all of this to discover new products, which I've added to my favourites after lots and lots of testing. When I launch a new product for a brand, I'll often include a swipe-up to where my Hinchers can buy that item, but I don't ever get any money from the actual sales. That would be crazy! The only affiliate schemes I'm part of currently are eBay and Shark where I make a small percentage of the sale price for the referral.

Zoflora is a good example in this case, I think. As you know, that little bottle was the product that started all of this off for me. I love Zoflora as much today as I did back then, and you will have seen me mention and show it count-less times on my stories. But I have never worked in paid partnership with Zoflora. They've sent me bottles of Springtime as gifts when I've run out, and all their new releases, which I just love receiving, but I've never been paid any money to promote their product. I rave about it as much as I do because I just love it. It really is as simple as that.

## 'Her house is too perfect to be real.
## It looks like a show home.'

I love a freshly Hinched house, but I can assure you, it is definitely not perfect. It's a normal family home, it's often messy and disorganised and it's definitely lived in. How could it not be with our Ronnie and Henry on the go all day every day around the house?

There are often times when my windows are grimy, when the skirting boards have gathered dust and when there are so many piles of washing you can't even see the carpet! Oh well. That's real life.

Believe it or not, I don't mind mess and I'm not obsessive about cleaning. Yes, I love to Hinch and it really helps me mentally, but it's not my number one priority in life. It never has been. I just enjoy it so much and that enjoyment sparks passion. So I'll happily admit I have a passion to clean, or rather, Hinch myself happy.

When Ronnie gets older I want our home to be a place his friends always feel welcome and I will fully embrace all of the mess that comes with that!

I keep on top of the cleaning as much as I can – little and often is what I've always found works best for me – but sometimes it might take me a couple of weeks to work through my Hinch List.

That's where my Ta-Daa lists come in handy! A list of extra jobs I've achieved during the day without really thinking about it is a reminder that even if I haven't ticked much off my main Hinch List, I've still managed to get stuff done.

So I do as much as I can. But pristine? Spotless? Absolutely no chance.

### 'She doesn't really clean her house – she has a professional cleaner.'

Sorry to disappoint you, guys, but I genuinely do it all myself. Why would I get someone else in to do it for me? Cleaning is one of the things I enjoy most in life!

A while back when this conspiracy theory made the papers, a journalist knocked on my neighbour's door and offered her money to get a picture of the professional cleaning van when it pulled up. You know, the one that didn't exist and was never coming.

I get on really well with my neighbours. They've known me since day one here, and the lady, bless her heart, turned around and told them to get lost.

I have never had a cleaner. The only help I have is that sometimes, if I'm run off my feet, my mum will come round and do some ironing for me, as a favour. That's it.

It's our toilet, and I'm going to be the one to pine it, thanks very much!

### 'Most of her followers are bought fake accounts.'

Honest to God, I wouldn't even know how you would go about buying followers. I don't have the first clue!

I know it's possible to do that now, because I asked my management what it was all about when I first saw someone comment that they thought I'd done that on one of my grid posts. And shortly after, Instagram did a clear-out when a load of celebs lost their bought followers and their followings went down by quite a bit. Firstly, my management explained to me that if they're looking to take someone on, that's one of the first things they check. And secondly, I hardly lost any of my followers during all of that, so that must tell those who doubt me something.

Apparently there are bot accounts out there, but you can't help it if they follow you. And if those accounts look suspicious or they haven't been used for a while, Instagram closes them down or clears them eventually.

I don't think people really think things through sometimes. If so many of my followers are fake, then who is buying my books?

### 'It's all run now by the Mrs Hinch team with very little input from Sophie.'

I wish! Wouldn't that be lovely, to let a whole team of people run the show for me while I sat back and relaxed with a cup of tea and a box of biscuits?

I don't wish that actually. Not at all. Seriously, though, even if that was possible, there's no way I could cope with it. I'd hate it.

I might lack self-confidence in a lot of areas and I have

never been good at putting myself forward, but when it comes to my Instagram, it is all me. And I am so protective of it! It's almost like I put my Mrs Hinch hat on and if anyone tries to influence me on what I need to say or do with it, I won't be swayed and I'm not interested.

It's strange, because in my everyday life, I'm hopeless when it comes to decision-making and always prefer listening to and following advice from other people.

I said from the very beginning that I wouldn't be a performing monkey or some sort of cash cow. I'm not a puppet. My team know to leave me alone to just get on with it, as much as they can, bless them, and I know they're always just a call away if I need any support.

I *know* my followers and I know what works, and the reason we have such a good relationship is because we understand each other and you guys allow me to be myself, completely and utterly. You'd see through it in an instant if someone was scripting my content or telling me what to do.

So I crack on doing what I do and most of the time, it just seems to work. And it's an amazing feeling.

### 'Using all those products means she's responsible for the climate crisis.'

I'm going to be perfectly honest here: before I sat down and watched the episode of *Blue Planet II* about plastics, I was very clueless. Like a lot of other people, I'd always recycled what I could and had a bit of awareness about climate change without really fully understanding it.

But watching that programme shocked me to my core and it made me bring big changes into our day-to-day life straightaway. It also made me feel like I desperately needed to know more and so I started doing lots of reading about what I could do to help, because it's terrifying what's happening to our beautiful planet.

The first thing I realised was that I wasn't sure what a lot of the recycling symbols on packaging really meant. I put a poll on my stories asking people what they thought the sign with the two green interlocking arrows was for and over 98,000 people got it wrong. They had thought the same as me – that the item could be recycled.

That's not the case. It actually means that the company who makes the product makes a financial contribution to recycling services in Europe, but not necessarily that the item itself can be recycled.

Confusing, right?

So there are a lot of us in the same boat here who need to rewind and go back to basics. I'm learning what all the symbols mean so I can be sure to dispose of everything in the right way and I'm using TerraCycle which is a brilliant scheme for collecting and repurposing non-recyclable waste.

You will probably have seen my labelled TerraCycle boxes on my stories (I love 'em!) and me and Jamie take a trip once a week to our local point to empty them.

I can't be completely plastic-free – I think most people would find that near on impossible – but what I can do is make sure every item leaves my house in the right way, whether that's recycling, through TerraCycle or passing it on elsewhere.

I'm learning all the time and I'm getting better and better each week. We are all learning, aren't we? I have an influential account and so I'm taking it seriously and using my position to spread the right messages. I think many people making a few small changes where they can will have a bigger impact than only a few people making absolutely all the necessary changes.

I focus on what I do in my house and show that example and go to bed knowing that I've done my best.

We all have a part to play and a responsibility to do our bit, but climate change wasn't caused by me buying a bottle of Zoflora.

**'It's all an act. She has nothing in common with her followers but pretends she's one of them.'**

My life might have changed but I have not. I shop in the same stores, I buy the same things, I eat the same food, I wear the same clothes and I have the same friends.

Something that I've heard before, which I'll be honest really got to me, was the fact that some people would say that I don't suffer from anxiety at all, and that I was using it as a way to seem more relatable to people. I won't go on about it too much here, because I've written a whole chapter about the anxiety I've struggled with my whole life. But to suggest I'd do something as low as to fake a mental illness in the hope of becoming more popular really amazes and also saddens me.

I chat with my followers all the time and I love connecting with you guys whether that's online or in person.

We laugh together, we cry together, we support each other, we lift each other up. I genuinely feel as if I'm talking to my friends. In fact, I have made friends through Instagram who I see in my day-to-day life, who I wouldn't ordinarily have met otherwise. You guys tell me all the time how much I help you. You have no idea just how much you help me too. As you know, I like to go to bed on a quote each and every night, and I receive thousands of messages from my followers saying that they really needed to read some of the quotes I posted that day. What you guys don't know is that I screenshot and save your lovely messages to read as a comfort to get me through on those days when I'm struggling too.

We are a big family and I know my followers don't begrudge me any of the success of Mrs Hinch because they helped to make it what it is today.

I will never forget where I started and nor will I forget the Hinchers whose love, loyalty and support put me here.

Wow, that felt quite good getting it all off my chest! Hopefully that's cleared a lot of things up, although my

Hinchers always know the truth and don't listen to any of the gossip. And I always say, if you hear something about me that you're not sure about, just ask me. Thank you — every single one of you — for knowing me, understanding me, accepting me and, most of all, for believing in me.

# Nine

## The Fame Game

The gossip and speculation, rumours and trolling seem to be part and parcel of a life in the spotlight these days. It feels a bit like everyone wants to be famous.

I think people see getting a shot at stardom as the golden ticket to a non-stop party lifestyle, being worshipped by millions and access to a quick and easy fortune. With all the reality TV shows (which I love, by the way!) and with how popular social media influencers are nowadays, it means anyone can give it a bloody good go now.

But what I'd say to the girls and boys hoping to get a place on programmes like *Love Island* or *Ex on the Beach* is to please give it a lot of thought, because it's not all it's cracked up to be. Guys, you are actually living your best life right now, you just don't realise it yet!

I worry about all the people coming off those shows and walking into a completely new life, one they know nothing about and have very little control over.

Before all this, I had an idea of what I thought fame was like. You know, a lot of living it up in business class, sipping champagne and general swanning about wearing diamonds and designer gear and posing on yachts in glamorous locations.

Now, I'm sure that if you're Kim Kardashian, there *is* a fair amount of that malarkey and there are definitely the most amazing perks which come from being 'known'.

But it's also a massive shock to the system and very unnerving coming to terms with no longer being anonymous and going so quickly from being someone nobody knows from Adam to a so-called 'celeb'. Especially for someone like me, a normal girl from a normal town who is very self-conscious and constantly worried about what other people think of her.

Goodness me, I'm literally the worst person for this Instagram thing to have happened to! It's not something I ever wanted or planned for, but here we are.

I just want people to know not to chase this life, and if it's something you really would love to do, think long and hard about it first and go in with your eyes wide open.

If I've learned one thing through this whole experience, it's to treasure the simple life and hold on to it as tight as you can.

Getting loads of Instagram likes and invitations to VIP parties might sound great to some, but to be perfectly honest, the few events I've been to have reminded me why I love being at home in my own space tucked away safely on my sofa.

The everyday things we normally all take for granted are actually what make life beautiful. Pub lunches with your family on a Sunday, walks in the field, pottering about in the garden, dancing around like no one's watching in your kitchen to cheesy music, ordering a takeaway with your mates or curling up on the sofa with the person you love.

That's what's precious, that's what matters.

I can't say I was ever into big nights out before all this anyway. I remember me and one of my friends went to my first (and last) music festival back in 2013. It was the We Are FSTVL in Upminster, Essex, and we got our tickets even though neither of us drank and we both have pretty bad social anxiety, so the build-up to going was huge for us. But we said to each other we were going to go to a festival and that's what we did.

I didn't have a clue what to wear so I googled 'festival outfits' to get some ideas, but oh dear God, whatever kind of 'look' I was going for, I'm pretty sure I didn't come close to pulling it off!

I had this bow wrapped round my head, a green rain mac, a little flowery dress, giant hoops in my ears and this big chain necklace. None of it went together and goodness knows who I was trying to be, but when we got there, everyone else looked so cool in such an effortless way. My attempt at festival chic just made me look stark raving mad.

I was so self-conscious that I ended up hiding behind my friend the whole time and when we got into the queue for the Portaloos I was actually glad to be stood there waiting for ages because it meant at least I wasn't 'on show' elsewhere.

I can laugh about it now, but I promise you, it wasn't even remotely funny at the time. I didn't know any of the songs, I didn't know how to dance – people were doing this shuffling thing which I couldn't get my legs to repeat for love nor money. They all looked like they were in this one massive girl band and belonged together and I was the backing singer who shouldn't have bothered showing up. It was so bad!

About halfway through the day I turned to my friend and said: 'Shall we go home?'

And to my huge relief, she said yes. So we grabbed a hotdog on the way out, her mum picked us up and that was our whole day. You live and learn, and I definitely learned that music festivals are not for me. There's no reason for that to change just because of Instagram so I'll carry on politely declining invites to the big events, as lovely as they are to receive.

A lot about my life is different, though, and it's something I'm very aware of. You know when Facebook flashes up those memories so you can see what you posted on that day five or six years ago? It always makes me feel very strange because it reminds me of the life I had before any of this happened. I definitely know what I've gained in the last few years and it's been amazing, but those memories remind me, to a certain extent, of what it is I've lost.

I live in the same house, I wear the same clothes, I haven't changed anything physically, but my life often doesn't feel that simple or straightforward any more.

I'm not a celebrity. I don't even like calling myself a 'public figure' – that sounds weird. I guess I'm a social media personality, and with that has come, well, fame.

Fame means I'm never alone, and wherever I go, there are friendly faces, which gives me a lovely warm feeling. My DMs are so incredible, they literally give me life.

Being known also means sometimes taking twice as long to get anything done – even a trip to the local shops can be a bit of a mission these days. If I pop into the village, I'm normally stopped for about twenty photos, which I don't mind at all. I love meeting you guys so much and you tell me that meeting me makes your day, and it's a special thing to be able to do that for someone, and if it means I have to include a bit more time to do whatever I'm doing, then that's the least I can do.

I see it as a real blessing that my job has connected me with so many lovely people.

Having said that, I do miss being able to run out to the Co-op in my slippers, my hair piled up and with no make-up on! Not that I'm worried about my followers seeing me, because I know they wouldn't give two hoots about any of that. But I'd hate for the press to get hold of a photo of me and the headlines the next day claim something ridiculous like Mrs Hinch was having a breakdown.

I'm pretty rubbish at being a celebrity. I don't go to parties or eat in Michelin-starred restaurants or shop in designer boutiques. We still get our weekly shop from Morrisons rather than buying posh food from pricey supermarkets and I'm more than happy to sit in my lounge eating spaghetti hoops out of a jug.

I remember me and Jamie decided to pop into the Charlotte Street Hotel in London one day for breakfast on the way to a meeting with my management. I'm not saying the food wasn't great – it was delicious smoked salmon and all the usual nice stuff – but when we got the £45 bill for what was a breakfast for two, I nearly fell off my chair. We could have gone to McDonald's and got a £4 McMuffin! How come the hash browns were three times the price of the ones in McDonald's? A potato's a potato, mate!

You guys know that I still go to B&M, Home Bargains and Poundland for my Hinch Hauls like I always have, and I love finding new bargs on eBay. That will never change.

On the odd occasion I have splashed out, I always feel terribly guilty afterwards. I remember going to Selfridges in Central London with Jamie, who suggested I treat myself to a smart new handbag.

If you've ever been to Selfridges, you'll know what a

beautiful shop it is; everything about it screams luxury, and to be honest, I felt like a fish out of water.

For a start, it was pouring with rain outside and I was carrying my umbrella in a little Wilko bag – my mum always told me 'keep a plastic bag on you for your umbrella' – but everyone in there had those big, glossy cardboard bags with the rope handles. My hair had been caught in the rain, I was head to toe in Primark and I felt like I was sticking out like a sore thumb.

Jamie could tell I was feeling a bit out of place and he said: 'Come on, you deserve to have your *Pretty Woman* moment, you've worked bloody hard for this!'

So off we went to Louis Vuitton and I tried to act like I totally knew what I was doing and came here all the time. I know this is going to make me sound like I was away with the fairies, but when the assistant approached us to see if we needed any help, I found myself trying to talk a bit differently. A little bit more well-spoken, upper class, you know?

And when I just happened to lean on the counter mid-conversation, I quickly stood up straight again, worried that leaning wasn't the 'done thing'. I just felt so awkward!

Some of the bags were up on the high shelves with a spotlight on them. I guessed they were the display items and the assistant would go and get you one from the hundreds they had out the back. But no. They are the actual ones.

There was one I fell in love with – a limited edition, it turns out. I kid you not, when I asked if I could have a look at it, the assistant put these silk gloves on, reached up to get this bag and brought it down so slowly I realised I was holding my breath. You could have cut the tension with a knife!

She gently unzipped it like it was alive and she started stroking it and moving it from left to right, showing it off like she was on *The Price is Right*! She basically groomed it for five minutes while I was stood there thinking: 'What is going off here?!' I actually had to stop myself from laughing.

To be fair, she must have done a great job of showing it off, because I thought it was the smartest bag I'd ever seen, but, guys, when I saw the price, I could have swallowed my tongue.

I was just about to say to Jamie 'Let's get out of here!', but I noticed the assistant looking me up and down. It was subtle and she probably didn't even realise herself she was doing it, but I definitely caught it. And it made me stop.

I looked a bit of a state from the rain and I was still holding my sodden umbrella in my little Wilko bag – I definitely didn't look like the put-together and wealthy customers she was probably used to serving and I could tell she was waiting for me to make my excuses because I couldn't afford it.

So in that moment, that split second, I thought 'screw you' and I got my card out.

'I'll take it, thank you,' I said, feeling a sudden rush of adrenaline.

In the heat of it all, I grabbed the matching purse for good measure and said: 'And I'll have that, too.'

Her face! Don't get me wrong, it wasn't that she'd not been nice to me, but it was obvious that she hadn't really taken me seriously. I reckon if I'd gone in there in a nice pair of Louboutins, a smart designer suit, my hair in a neat bun and been all 'good afternoon', they probably would have flocked around me and treated me very differently.

People are so quick to judge.

That bag purchase is something I can laugh at now and I'm glad I got my 'moment', but I will also regret it forever because of the amount of money it cost. After we checked out, we got in the lift to go back to the car and Jamie asked if I was pleased with it.

'No!' I said. 'I feel awful!'

He looked at me like I was mad, but all I wanted to do was chuck the bag out the lift and pretend it had never happened. I spent the whole journey home feeling ill about having blown all that money on a bloody bag.

I've only dared use it a handful of times. I have little leather wipes for it and I enjoy cleaning it and keeping it all nice. And if I have a meeting, I take it with me and carefully place it on the table, to show it off. It's even got little feet on the bottom of it! But most of the time it just sits in my wardrobe and I stare at it and say: 'I'm not going to bin you, but Christ, you cost me a lot of money!'

Fancy bags just aren't practical when you're a mum, anyway. I can't fit my nappies and wipes in there, so Ronnie's changing bag is my day-to-day handbag now.

It's not a waste, though, because it's something I can pass on to my niece when she gets older and there will always be a story behind it. But I will not be buying another designer handbag for as long as I live. I can't take the drama!

The thrill of finding a cheap eBayer gets me going way more than an over-priced handbag.

And meeting you guys is always way more inspiring and exciting to me than being introduced to some celebrity off the telly. While I'm so happy that there are so many Hinchers who feel able to stop me for a photo and a chat, I know there are lots of others who are too shy to say anything.

Earlier this year I was having a coffee in Costa when a lady came up to my table and placed a little handwritten note down before running off in a hurry.

She'd written: 'Mrs Hinch. I don't want to disturb your lunch but just wanted to say you've really helped me through a tough time while being signed off work. Thank you for all you do.'

She'd signed it 'a local Hincher', but she'd gone before I'd had the chance to read it. If I'd been able to catch her, I would have given her the biggest and tightest of hugs. I just wish I'd got to give her a squeeze and say thank you.

I put it on my stories and I hope she saw it, because I can't tell you how touched I was.

I get recognised in the oddest of places. When we were in the Maldives on our honeymoon, we were on a golf buggy heading to the restaurant for lunch.

I see these influencer types on holiday looking like beauty queens, walking around with their big sunglasses and their hair and make-up done perfectly.

Hinchers, I'm not like that. My hair was wet with sweat, my face was greasy, I had my fake Celine sunglasses on and my legs were stuck to the seat because I was so hot. Believe me, there was nothing 'influential' about that particular look.

But someone saw me and called out: 'Mrs Hinch! Mrs Hinch!'

I almost turned around on instinct. But I felt such a mess that I decided to pretend I hadn't heard. I know that sounds really awful, but I just couldn't do it. The same lady approached me again that night at dinner and I went over and said hi – I felt a bit more presentable by that time.

There was another funny evening when Jamie and I went to London's West End to see the stage show of *Mary Poppins*. It was our first night out as a couple after Ronnie was born so we were really looking forward to it. We were like a couple of over-excited kids let loose for the night.

Central London on a Saturday night is always buzzing with people going here, there and everywhere and so never in a million years did I expect to get spotted. But I did.

I got stopped for pictures on the way into the theatre, inside the auditorium, during the interval and then again on our way out. But the most bonkers thing of all was that the cast caught wind I was in and Zizi Strallen, the girl playing Mary Poppins, is a dedicated Hincher, God love her!

Apparently, they all give their costumes a little spray of Zoflora after each performance to keep them fresh: be still, my beating heart!

Zizi mentioned me on her stories and I became a total fangirl for the evening. It was a real dream of a night but also one of those times we both found completely surreal. How is this even happening to us? How is this our life?

I think it was our trip to Disneyland Paris for my thirtieth birthday earlier this year that really brought home to me just how much this Insta-fame has changed my life.

I'd not been abroad on holiday since our honeymoon, and so when people spotted me in the park on the first day, it took me by surprise. I know it might sound weird, but at first, I quite naively thought it must have just been a one-off coincidence.

But the second half of our stay was during half-term and once that started and the place got busier, oh my gosh, it was a different kettle of fish entirely. I couldn't actually get from one ride to the next without being stopped, which was so lovely, because at the end of the day, I'm in this position because of my followers, but it also made getting around the park slightly tricky at times!

They'd run up saying 'hiya, Soph!' (it's not really Mrs Hinch these days – everyone just calls me Soph and I love that), and they were asking if I was missing Henry, how Ronnie was doing and saying well done for getting here in one piece because they'd seen me stressing over all the suitcase-packing on my stories.

When one person takes a photo, other people notice and start coming over to see what the fuss is about and usually within a couple of minutes, we'd end up with a bit of a queue. It was only ever love and loveliness, but I was taken aback.

Disneyland, bless them, must have picked up on it and they very kindly gave us one of their guides who tell you where everything is so you're not standing with the map working out which direction to go in, which is when you're more likely to get spotted. That helped us keep moving through the crowds and unnoticed when we needed to get somewhere quickly.

We brought my mum and niece over to join us halfway through, and one thing I worried about was my niece getting caught up in the Mrs Hinch madness when I wanted her to be able to make the most of all the rides.

She was actually asked on a few occasions to take the photo, but it was fine and it was the best feeling to know I could pay for my family to have a trip like this, staying in the famous Disneyland Hotel. The truth is, we could have got the whole trip for free, all expenses paid. But it was important to me that we paid our way, full price, for everything.

It was the absolute holiday of a lifetime. You know when you're a child and you literally have no idea of the fact there is badness in the world and everything is pure and innocent and beautiful? Well, that's how it felt.

From the moment you step out of the hotel and you hear the Disney music in the park, you're transported to another world.

It was a comforting feeling of nostalgia, like when you smell the perfume your mum used to wear when you were little or you hear the song that reminds you of your first love and it gives you goose bumps.

I threw myself into it and went full-on Disney. It's got to be done, hasn't it? I bought a Disney tracksuit and I had my Mickey ears on the whole time. I even bought an autograph book which was full by the end of the trip from getting all the characters to sign – I was just like a kid again! It was pure escapism and most of the time I forgot all about being a grown-up.

Everyone there was so happy and kind to each other and it was just the perfect place for my thirtieth celebrations. I'd kept it secret on my Instagram about where I was going until the last minute, because I thought it would be interesting to see where people guessed I'd choose for my big birthday.

Lots of people assumed Dubai with all the VIP areas and bottles of champagne and tiny bikinis. But amazing as that might sound for some, it's my actual worst nightmare. I couldn't think of anything I'd rather do less, so that was never on my radar.

Other people thought it was New York or the Maldives, but both of those are too far to go with Ronnie and my anxiety was already through the roof thinking of taking him out of the country at all, let alone going long haul.

For Ronnie's first holiday I wanted to be far enough away to have left the country, but not so far that I wasn't sleeping for worrying about it. So Disneyland Paris was the perfect place.

He was only eight months at the time and I didn't think he would understand that much when he was there, but he was really taking in all the lights and the noises and the characters. He was holding their hands and they were cuddling him and holding him – these characters are really big and they're right in your face and he wasn't bothered at all. He found it all really funny and I was so proud of him.

Some people asked why I didn't use the time to have a complete break from Instagram, but you are part of my life now so obviously you guys were coming along.

If I'd followed someone and watched their whole journey to the point where they could afford a holiday like that only for them to then say 'OK, see you later, I'm not showing you anything', I'd be like, 'Er, hang on a minute, mate!'

I couldn't not speak to my Hinchers on my birthday and I had to show you all Ronnie's first holiday. I wanted to take you with me and I'm so glad I was able to share the joy of it with you all. Over 1.5 million people watched my stories showing the light show and you were messaging saying how you felt you were there with me and thanking me for taking you on the trip. How amazing is that?

I will always have time for my Hinchers – you guys must know that by now! When people approach me, even though we've never met, I always know we're going to get along and have a lovely chat.

What I'm not so comfortable about, and again, this is one of the downsides of being known, is being secretly filmed by people on their phones. That's just not OK and it feels very creepy to me.

No longer having privacy and the freedom to go about your day unnoticed is something you don't appreciate until it's taken away.

Earlier this year I was on my way to Brussels for a big meeting with P&G when I spotted someone taking a video of me at St Pancras station. It was an early train at the crack of dawn and I'd not long woken up so wasn't exactly looking my best.

I politely said to the lady filming: 'Oh hi, would you like a photo?'

And do you know what she replied?

She said: 'No, no, it's fine – I don't look that great today!' I mean, neither did I, but she carried on filming me.

I genuinely have no words for that.

There have been plenty of bizarre incidents like that which you do have to brush off and laugh about in the grand scheme of things. I don't think people mean any harm by it – it's just thoughtless, really – but it can be really degrading and make me feel that I'm there for public viewing.

One night me and Jamie were in a restaurant having a meal and a lady came up to us while we were eating. It was a very rare date night for us and we obviously just wanted to enjoy our roast chicken and Appletiser (I do love an Appletiser!) but she was apologetic and said: 'I'm so sorry to interrupt your meal, I'd just like to take a photo.'

I smiled, said no worries and went to move round next to her for the selfie.

And she looked at me and said: 'Oh no, I meant a picture just of you two!'

She actually wanted to take a photo of me and Jamie eating our dinner! I think Jamie and I were both too gobsmacked to respond for a couple of seconds before I told her very nicely that I was more than happy to have a photo with her, but a picture of me and my husband out on a date night, mid-meal, just didn't feel right.

Anyway, me and her had a selfie together and then I started stressing about her going off and badmouthing me to everyone and saying I was a stuck-up cow for refusing the first photo. It really is a minefield, but I feel like I do have to have some boundaries.

It's always lovely to meet my Hinchers – if you ever see me, please come and say hi as I love nothing more than meeting you guys – but being in the public eye has also brought with it a level of press interference I won't ever be comfortable with. Yes, I put a lot of my life on social media, but I don't think that should mean I am up for grabs 24/7 while I'm going about my day.

My first real encounter with the paparazzi was when I was about five months pregnant and went to the hairdresser's. As I pulled out of my street, I noticed there was a big black van behind me – I was going to Brentwood, which is a good half an hour's drive away, and it followed me the whole way there.

I could see him in my rear-view mirror and it was making me feel panicky, my mind racing between wondering what the hell he wanted from me and telling myself it was just my imagination working overtime.

But when I arrived at the salon, I watched him park up, wind down the window and sure enough, I saw the camera. My heart dropped.

The feeling of being followed by a strange man when you're a pregnant woman on your own is terrifying. I ran into the hairdresser's and in all the distress of that moment, my reaction was extreme. I called my management and I said I wanted Instagram gone.

ONNIE JAMES GEORGE HINCHLIFFE
20TH JUNE 2019
THE DAY OUR LIVES
CHANGED FOR THE BETTER

OUR RONNIE ROO

Ronnie's FIRST Christmas Dinner 2019

YOU'VE GOT A FRIEND IN ME

AND THEN, ALONG CAME...

Born IN 2021

i'm new here

LENNIE ALAN JAMES HINCHLIFFE
22ND MAY 2021

HINCH
BROS

BEHIND THE SCENES COVER PHOTOSHOOT
WITH LOVE FROM OUR LITTLE FAMILY TO YOUR
XX

I told her: 'I want everything stopped, get rid of the contracts, get rid of everything. I can't do this any more, I'm out.'

I've often asked myself whether this was definitely the kind of life I wanted, but this was the first time it was brought to a head. Shaking and crying, I switched off my phone. I didn't want to be contacted by anyone. My management immediately phoned Jamie who jumped straight in a taxi and came to the salon. When he got there, he was furious about what had happened, but he held me close and calmed me down.

I'd managed to get the number plate of the van and my management were all systems go, to be fair. They were able to track down which picture agency he was from and issued a warning that if he or any of their other photographers were ever to follow me again, we would sue.

After I'd had time to think about it, I decided I wasn't going to let one horrible experience take away everything I'd worked hard for and everything that me and the Hinchers had built together.

So I took a few days off and came back again, although I felt a lot more wary about everything. I've never seen that particular guy since, but it wasn't the last time I'd feel violated by a pap.

It was a few days after I'd had Ronnie and I had to go to my car to get something. I was still in a lot of pain from giving birth and feeling quite fragile, but I noticed a slate-grey van parked in a funny position at the end of the road. Then I saw the long lens camera zooming in on me.

The thought of a strange man lurking outside my house, waiting for me to come out so he could take photos of me without my permission . . . it turns my stomach.

I was on the phone to my management again and said: 'It's happening again – I can't leave my house. This is going to make me ill.'

We got the police involved that time. They moved him on and gave me a number to call if it ever happened again and as far as I know, nobody has been camped outside my house since. Having that number has given me a bit of reassurance, just knowing that I have somewhere and someone to turn to, but it didn't make me feel any less scared.

We've worked so hard for this house and I love it. It's my home and it should be my safe space, but at that point I felt so devastated, moving away felt like the only option. I remember looking at tiny little Ronnie and thinking: 'Oh God, he has no idea that I've brought him into this mad, mad world.'

That's when Jamie took charge of the situation and we packed our bags and headed off around Suffolk for a few weeks where no one could find us.

I have to consider things now that would never even have crossed my mind before. Bringing Ronnie home when he was first born, for example. All new parents are excited for that moment they're allowed to leave the hospital and put their baby in the car seat for the first time, to take them home. We had to plan for the fact that there might have been press outside the hospital waiting to take a photo.

At that point I hadn't even announced the birth on Instagram and I wanted to be the one to share our news with my followers at a time that felt right for us as a family. It was my maternal instinct kicking in and the need to protect Ronnie at all costs, and I was also in agony, still recovering from his birth and the stitches I'd had to have. I didn't want any photos of Ronnie or me and Jamie published all over the press.

So, we worked it out like a military operation and Mum took Ronnie out in the seat with the hood down and got him into the car. I walked down with my sister in my hat and big coat and Jamie came down separately with all the bags, because if me and him are together, we're instantly recognised.

We managed it and the paps didn't get their shot, which was the main thing, but I felt a bit of sadness. Where was our moment? It felt so planned, stripped of any joy, excitement or emotion.

I guess it's just one of those things we have to accept now, a sacrifice that comes with a job I love so much but which has turned our way of life upside down.

I saw a lot of messages and comments speculating on which magazine exclusive we were going to do our big first baby reveal photos in. We declined all the offers we received because we've never been interested in any of that. I know a lot of people do choose to introduce their baby to the world in that way, but that's just not us. We wanted all of it to be in our way, on our own terms.

We've had to rethink a lot about how we live day to day and change to a new way of doing things.

We used to love going on all-inclusive holidays, somewhere with guaranteed sunshine and not too far away. That was perfect for us and we enjoyed being in one place where you've got your food sorted, the pool during the day and your entertainment in the evening.

My mum and dad used to take me and my sister to all-inclusives when we were kids and we'd have the best time. We'd go to places like Lanzarote and Tenerife where we'd meet friends and be in and out of the pool all day, doing water aerobics and splashing around.

As we got older, me and Sam would feel really grown up leaving Mum and Dad to do their own thing and going off and getting lunch together because it was all within the safety of one big complex. I have nothing but amazing memories of our family holidays.

What with Mrs Hinch taking off and Ronnie coming along, we never managed to get away abroad last year, so Jamie and I promised ourselves we'd get something booked for this summer. This was at the start of the year before the Coronavirus crisis and, as it turned out, we couldn't have gone anywhere anyway, but when I sent him some all-inclusive hotels to check out, he just looked at me like I was mad.

He said: 'We can't do that any more, Soph.'

He said it would be impossible. I asked him what he meant.

'Babe, people would be coming up to you around the pool, approaching you in the restaurant, wanting to see Ronnie, and it wouldn't ever feel like we could relax. We'd never have a meal on our own as a family.'

I knew he was right. And then seeing how things were in Disneyland proved it.

It made me a bit emotional when I realised that it was something from my old life that I'd lost. Instead, Jamie went online and found some private villas with walled pools so we'd be on our own, with no risk of being photographed or filmed, and I'd even be able to lie there topless if I wanted to. (Not that I would, but yanno.)

I know to a lot of people a private villa might sound like an absolute dream, and of course it is. But I couldn't get over thinking: 'What about my boy?'

Of course, Ronnie's got us, but I want him to enjoy the social side of holidays and have the experiences I did as a kid. What fun is he going to have stuck in a villa with only us for company? I want him to make little friends!

But then Jamie flipped it round and asked me what quality of holiday Ronnie would have if his mummy was stopping for photos with people. So, we've had to change our idea of what a holiday means to us and although the lockdown put a stop to any travel plans we had this summer, next year we're hoping to book a villa and fly all my family out as well so Ronnie will have lots of people to play with.

I can see that with the way things are right now, it's best for Ronnie. It's really important that when I'm with my baby, he gets all of me. For instance, I take him swimming once a fortnight and we pay for a private session in our local pool. It's not that I don't want to swim with other people, but I need to be 100 per cent focused on my boy. He deserves that and I just want to be a mummy, swimming with her son for a while, rather than being Mrs Hinch.

Please don't take this the wrong way. I'm not moaning, because I'm truly grateful for all the incredible upsides that come with fame. But I do think it's OK to feel a bit sad sometimes. I can love my life and be excited about the future while at the same time missing some of the old life I've had to leave behind and will never get back.

I sometimes feel like I'm in a cage – that's the best way I can explain it.

I have six best friends who I introduced you to in my first book – my kids, as I call them and have done since school – and we've never been closer. But sometimes when I see them, I get upset because I look at their lives and I think: 'Wow, that's what mine could have, would have, should have been.'

I hope that makes sense. It's not a complaint, it's just something I notice, am aware of and feel.

My friends' love and support have been there since our schooldays, but it's never been more valuable to me than the last two years. When we're together, we never talk about Mrs Hinch or anything like that. We talk about Christmas shopping, how the kids are and what foods they're eating, how they're sleeping, *Love Island*, funny things and memories of school. Just normal conversations where I can switch off.

I have experience in the celeb world now, but I couldn't care less about showbiz goss and neither could they. I'd much rather sit with my mates having a Chinese and laughing our heads off just like we've done since forever.

I don't tag them in my stories, because if I did they might get unwanted attention, and I just want to protect them. This is my world not theirs and I don't want my best friends ever feeling any of the pressure I do some days.

If they've got a professional page, like Trace and her nails business, of course I'll share that, but their personal accounts stay private. They don't ask for it, they don't want it.

This is still all so new to me and I'm just learning on the go. God knows if I'm doing it right. There's certainly no instructions or Idiot's Guide to Fame!

I'm still trying to find the right balance – what to share and what to hold back. To go from being a very normal girl with a settled, ordinary life, to suddenly a lot of people knowing who I am and everything about me, has been tricky at times.

Accepting there's a chance that things will never be the same again is harder still.

But with my Hinchers by my side, the support of my family and friends, I'm definitely learning to live with it.

Being famous might not be my most favourite thing about all of this, but I understand that it goes hand in hand with what I do. I can't have one without the other, and the good which has come out of the last couple of years outweighs the bad and I never let myself forget that.

The friendships I've built with you guys and knowing that I'm making a difference – however small – to your lives is the reason I carry on. And although it's massively over-rated and not a path I'd ever choose, having a taste of fame has actually meant I know more than ever what is important.

For me, the key to being happy is keeping things as normal as possible. This is one of the reasons why I don't accept many gifted pieces in my home any more. I am incredibly grateful for all the lovely companies who kindly want to send me their beautiful items. But you'll notice that I've kept hold of a lot of my original things because, as you know, I'm a firm believer in if it ain't broke, don't fix it. (Though I do love a good upcycle.) I don't want to replace pieces that are perfectly decent because I want to hold on tight to those parts of our home that remind me of my life before. I'm the same with my clothes. I enjoy organising what I've got and packing things away for next year. When I'm having one of my more anxious days, I like to fish out my oldest and most favourite loungewear set, get comfy and remind myself that I'm still me. I'm still just Soph.

The closer I stay to the super ordinary life I had before all of this, the better I feel.

# Ten

# How the Industry Works

If someone told me a few years ago that my career would be working in social media I'd have looked at them like they'd actually lost the plot.

I'd always enjoyed sites like Facebook and MSN (anyone else remember that? Old school!) and I was starting to feel my way round Instagram, but it was only ever a bit of fun to me; a way of staying in touch with the people I loved and sharing things that made me smile.

I didn't understand much about 'the digital age' outside of that – for me, it was never about showing off my life, or anything I had, and I certainly didn't know anything about what an influencer actually was or what they did. And to think now I apparently am one. I just find it really strange. Plus I've never been overly keen on the word 'influencer' if I'm perfectly honest. I never intended on influencing anyone. I just go about my normal life, work only with brands I love, and share those things on my account. I remember not that long ago I was in the optician's when the lady doing my eye test asked me what my occupation was. I froze because I didn't know what to say. I mean, what even is my job title? So I just said I work in the social media industry in the home section! She couldn't have looked more confused if she tried. You and me both, darling!

Even now I'm still learning new things every single day.

I know a lot of people think I get paid millions of pounds for not doing very much at all and there's a general opinion that the whole 'influencing' job is all about getting freebies. Which it really isn't; at least not in my experience anyway.

I'm fortunate enough to earn a very good income from being on Instagram and from my books, but it's never been about the money for me. It's way more about the community and the friendships. It feels odd to me to call it work because it doesn't even feel like work most of the time because I love it so much!

But at the same time, it's not a walk in the park either. This is a full-time, 24/7 job for me and there is a lot more to it than people realise. If I'm not recording stories or testing out products, I'm thinking up and creating new ideas and trying to think of ways to keep my account fresh and uplifting, which I really hope it is.

I write out my Hinch List, which is made up of the things I'd like to get done over the next week (or however long it takes) and that's what I work from. It's not set up or staged. I don't chuck dust around deliberately to clean up. It's all real, and that's what I do. My platform is my creation, a million per cent.

In between all of that, I spend a lot of time working on my books, which I really enjoy, and that includes regular catch-ups and progress updates with my team at Penguin, my publishers. So much goes into the life cycle of getting a book from start to finish. It's crazy. I had no idea. I feel so incredibly lucky to be able to be involved in the process, and it's amazing to see your ideas and your thoughts go from an idea in your head on to the page. It's something I'll never take for granted and it's another thing I have you guys to thank for.

I also have a lot of meetings with my management and with the brands I have contracts and partnerships with. I work hard to deliver well-thought-out content and I make sure I learn about products I love inside and out. It has to be more than just liking the smell of something (although that *is* very important to me, as you know!). It's so fascinating to me to understand the science behind why all the products I use and love work as well as they do. I love learning behind-the-scenes stuff, yanno, from the ingredients and performance power to the background of that business and how it all came about. I read up on all the safety dos and don'ts and I make notes, which I type up and file away. I have my own product bibles which I refer to all the time because I feel I have a duty to everyone watching me to make sure whatever I'm saying is accurate and safe.

My account is my baby, my pride and joy.

Take Flash, which I've used for years, for example. They may want me to tell my followers about a new formula and so I think about how I want to create that content and deliver it in a fun way to my followers. I am never told what to do beyond 'don't do this story in the nude' (haha, as if!) and 'don't swear' (occasionally a possible risk).

Seriously, though, all of it is up to me right down to where I stand and where I film it, what scenario I choose to set up, what tools I choose to use with the product, and so on. There's no camera crew, no lighting equipment, it's just me and my mobile phone which nine times out of ten has a crack down the screen because I've dropped it so many times while trying to Hinch one-handed, which is actually a lot trickier than it might seem!

While I am paid well for the work I do, I'd hate for people to think I'm rinsing this.

One of the questions I get asked a lot is how I decide who I'm going to work with. My management team handle the offers that come in and they pull together a list of the companies who have approached them about me. I then sit down, look at the list, consider each and every brand and say yes or no.

Brands I love like Minky, Scrub Daddy, P&G, Pampers, DFS, Carpetright, B&M, etc were all very easy yeses for me. I was like, 'Are you kidding me?' when I saw those names and I didn't even need to think about any of them. I was in awe that these companies wanted to work with me.

My followers place a massive amount of trust in me and I would never do anything to put that at risk, which is why I won't work with brands I haven't tried or don't know or believe in. And the products I talk about on my account are always affordable and the ones I believe are the best in the business.

Money has never been a deciding factor for me and it never will be. You would not believe how many offers I turn down. In fact, I turn down far more offers than I ever accept – and I'm very clear about what I draw the line at. I got offered a lot of money from a magazine to do a photoshoot with Ronnie when he was born but I've always declined anything like that.

I was once offered a very large sum of money to promote a range of vacuum cleaners, but I've always used Sharks (our Sharon, Shawn and Shelley!) and they've never let me down. Shark was also one of the first companies to approach me when I was starting out, and loyalty counts for a lot with me.

I've actually said a polite *no thank you* to the four biggest offers I've ever had. I could have taken the money and run, but I've rejected them for different reasons, whether that's been a conflict of interest with other brands I'm already working with or it's just not felt right. There have been baby brands I've declined because it felt too personal, and I mentioned earlier about clothing deals I've said no to because it would have involved modelling the clothes and that's *so* not my scene. The thought of it literally makes me go cold!

I expect a lot of you will have seen that BBC documentary last year when they set up and secretly recorded a few influencers and reality stars accepting deals to endorse a fake diet drink that contained cyanide. Cyanide! People like that don't seem to care about whether a product might be dangerous. They don't read into how the product they are endorsing is made because it seems like they are more interested in the money.

The influencers exposed on that documentary are still working and still have income rolling in. That just doesn't make sense. Integrity is one of the most important things to me. I think once people lose faith in you, and believe you're no longer telling the truth, you've lost them for good, and no amount of money is ever worth losing people's trust over as far as I'm concerned. And I will always stand by that.

I see people blatantly ignoring the advertising rules all the time and it really upsets me, because there are a lot of us out there who are desperately doing everything we can to follow all of the ever-changing regulations.

In an industry that is so open to abuse, of course it's right that what influencers share and how they share it is monitored. If we are being paid by a company to promote a product then we should be open and honest about that, and if we've received something as a gift, I agree we should make that clear. What I will say about both of those two points, however, is that because I only ever work with companies and brands that I completely believe in and support, whether I work with them on a paid or on a gifting basis, neither of those things change my opinion on a product or a service. The only things that make their way on to my account are things that I absolutely love. And nothing is ever going to change that.

The Advertising Standards Authority is the body who looks after all of this and they are definitely needed, but it's by no means a perfect system. The rules are constantly being updated, and every time they are, it's a bit like starting a new job and having to learn a different way of working. It can be hard to keep up!

Sometimes it feels like the accounts who continually stick two fingers up to the rules go unchallenged while others who really, really try can still find themselves in the firing line. I completely understand that it is their job to investigate reports that are brought forward to them, and I've always felt that they've dealt with anything to do with me fairly.

One of the most stressful periods of my life came in 2018 when I was reported to the ASA for apparently failing to follow all of the rules.

From when I was a kid, I've never been a rebel or a rule-breaker and still I found myself under investigation after spraying my sofa with a bottle of Febreze. I didn't realise at the time, but even though I'd bought the Febreze myself from B&M and wasn't paid by P&G to do that specific post, I should have labelled the post as an advert because Febreze is made by P&G who I am a brand ambassador for.

It was a genuine mistake on my part and I was mortified, but because it was formally reported the ASA had to look into it.

All the papers had these headlines about Mrs Hinch being investigated, and for about three weeks, the ASA went through all of my posts looking for evidence of any wrongdoing.

I can only describe that time as pure hell for me. I felt scared and I felt like a criminal, when all I'd done was spray my sofa with my Febreze! I thought my followers would lose trust in me and the critics would have won.

Although it was quickly identified that I had no case to answer and the investigation was dropped, that bit was never reported (apart from one small piece in the *Telegraph*), and to this day it feels like the allegations have been left hanging there with people thinking I'd deliberately gone against ASA guidelines.

These days, I am almost obsessive about how I tag my posts and I'm so petrified of getting it wrong, I often just put 'ad' to cover all bases!

If I do a swipe-up to eBay, I mark it as 'ad', but that's to declare the fact that I use affiliate links, which means I get a small percentage of the sale for my referral if traffic from my link ends up in a purchase.

Most brands offer these affiliate programmes now and absolutely anyone can sign up to them if they meet the criteria. Once an account has 10,000 followers on Instagram that unlocks the ability to post swipe-up links to your stories.

eBay and Shark are the only affiliates I'm with and I earn an income from them both each month. eBay, in particular, I love. I enjoy finding affordable items that either look amazing or are useful. I only ever recommend things I've bought and love myself. They are things I've spent time looking for to use or display in my home; random, affordable, funny and useful items. Absolute bargs like my baby caddies, my radiator covers, my under-the-sink storage shelves and my baskets which people see in my house all the time.

When it comes to gifting, I totally get that it's a mad concept to most people and it must be annoying to see certain influencers receiving piles of stuff they clearly don't need, for free.

Personally, I want to earn my belongings by working hard for them. I don't want to walk around my house and feel like I'm on a TV set – I can afford to pay for my things, so why shouldn't I?

If there are items I love and can share to help boost small businesses, then I will gratefully accept them and do just that.

For instance, anyone who follows me knows I love a wax melt. I have them all over my house and they're my favourite. I've always got mine from Ava May Aromas and I've shared Hannah's details on my page since the beginning. In the space of two years, she's gone from being a one-woman band to having twenty-three employees and seven workshops. She doesn't charge me for wax melts, but she's never paid me a penny for sharing her business and neither have I asked her to.

I've been offered deals with huge wax melt and home fragrance companies, but I've always stuck with Hannah from Ava May because she's a small business and I love her products and what she does.

If I get sent something like the medical baby box I shared a while back, which is such a fab idea, I'll tell my followers about it. I shared that box once and she sold out as a result.

The guys we got our lovely bath boards from are now doing it full-time and have been in touch to thank me for that.

People assume that everything in my house is gifted, but most of the items I buy myself, and I pay businesses and tradespeople even when they've offered things to me for free. We could have got a lot of our extension done for nothing, but we paid for it in full because anything less than that just wouldn't have sat comfortably with me.

And take the incredibly talented Matt who did my amazing space tidy and has had a lot of business off the back of that. When I went to him again to do my garage, he said he'd do it without charge but I wouldn't hear of it. I told him I wanted to pay, he said fine and I felt better for it.

Then there was Mr Loft Ladder. That was sheer madness! I tagged him in my stories when he came to fit our ladder because I think the telescopic design is a bloody good idea when you haven't got much space. I paid full price for it, asked my followers to show him some love and in the space of twenty-four hours he went from a handful of followers to over 30,000 and business has been booming ever since.

While I hugely appreciate everything people take the time to send me, I can't accept and share it all. I only have one house and there's only one Ronnie and I can't start changing him ten times a day just to show off different outfits.

But nothing goes to waste and most of it is either returned or goes to another good home. My team do an amazing job of helping me sort everything and we send a lot to charity – most of the beauty stuff goes to women's refuges. I take bags and bags of clothes to the baby bank down the road which is a fantastic thing to be able to do.

I try to ask people not to personalise the clothes they send for Ronnie because then that makes it much harder to pass them on.

Having people wanting to give you things for free is a very privileged position to be in, but I have had some quite unpleasant experiences from it, too.

Some gifters think that because they have sent me

something I am obliged to share it, and if I don't, I can sometimes be subjected to some pretty horrendous abuse. But I've been sent these things without me ever asking to receive them.

'I've sent you this item and you've never shared it. I knew you were fake, you awful woman' – that sort of thing, which can be upsetting when it pops up on my screen without warning.

One encounter was particularly bad. This guy turned up unannounced and uninvited at my house with some garden furniture. It was all personalised with Mrs Hinch but I didn't need it because we already have perfectly decent garden furniture.

He said: 'Well, I've personalised it so I can't give it to anyone else.'

I asked him how he'd got my address and he said he'd just worked it out.

If Jamie had been there, he would have said firmly: 'Thank you for the kind gesture but we're not accepting it. Please put it back in the van and leave.'

But I was on my own in the house and I was holding Ronnie who was still very little, so I wasn't about to have an argument with someone on the doorstep. And so the guy just left it there in my front garden.

Two weeks later I got the most disgusting messages saying: 'How dare you not share all that hard work I put into making you this furniture! Why the hell haven't you shared my page?'

The abuse I got was unbelievable. I was sitting there reading all this in floods of tears, looking at the furniture and just wanting it gone. Jamie snapped. He packed it up and took it away, and when he came back he said: 'It doesn't matter where it's gone, I've sorted it.'

Maybe he took it back to them, I don't know. He'd never tell me.

I felt like I'd been invaded in my own home. The thought of that man tracking me down to where I lived made me feel very vulnerable.

I have a PO Box which is where most items go to, but somehow people like him have managed to get hold of my address. I can't share anything that has been sent directly to the house because as soon as I put anything on a story with an account tagged, everyone goes to them and asks how they got their product to Mrs Hinch. If it was something that had been sent to my home, my address would be shared again, and while I'm in no way ungrateful, for our personal safety I just can't do it.

It's a funny old game though, isn't it? While I'm totally living the dream as far as jobs go, it is a lot more complicated and involved than it might first seem, but I hope that's helped pull back the curtain and make a little sense of what I admit is a very strange industry indeed.

I know there is a lot more that goes on behind the scenes with my account; stuff that even I'm not aware of because I purposely try not to get involved too much in the technical and statistics side of things. I can see how many people have followed and unfollowed and that's it.

Engagement, insights and all that, I stay away from and leave to my management to look after. I'd rather not know, mainly because I don't want to get sucked into checking all the time, because that's not what I'm about.

I will continue to be open and honest and I will carry on being selective about who I work with and what I choose to promote.

Mainly, I just want to focus on being part of this amazing little Insta world we've built, working hard for my brands, playing by the rules and sharing my best finds, most helpful tips and day-to-day life with my Hinchers.

And I will only ever be myself, because that's all I can and ever want to be.

# Eleven

# Growing Our Home

When I look around our Hinch house today I sometimes struggle to believe it's actually ours. It really is the house we always dreamed of and it is exactly how I always imagined our forever home to look.

Now, I'm not saying for one second that it's the best house on Instagram or that I'm some sort of interior designer – believe me, I know my style isn't to everyone's taste. And that's fine! Jeez, how boring would the world be if we all liked the same things?

But it's somewhere we've poured our heart and soul into and to me it's our very own little palace.

If you've been following me for a while, you'll know we had an extension done last year going from three bedrooms to four, building a bigger lounge and landing and giving us a much-wanted dining room. It's been everything we hoped it would be and more.

For a new-build property our garden is big, and that is one of the main reasons we picked this plot off plan – there was room to extend. We always dreamed of growing our home as soon as we planned to start a family, and it hit me that our dream had finally come true. On Christmas Day last year we were able to have fifteen members of our family sitting in our beautiful new dining room, eating the dinner we prepared. Well, my mum and sister cooked 99 per cent of it and I was more of a kitchen assistant, fetching and carrying dishes. That's about as much as they let me touch. I don't think they trusted me much with the food and precious turkey.

That's exactly what Christmas should be all about, and having both sides of the family coming together like that simply wouldn't have been possible in the past. But thanks to the extension, we now have the space for everyone and it meant the world to me and Jamie to be able to do that for Ronnie's first Christmas. Memories we'll cherish forever.

The idea behind growing our home was always so we could fill it with family and friends – all the people we love the most – and to see that vision become an actual reality was more emotional than I thought it would be.

I wanted everything to be perfect and spent months planning it all, right down to the last detail, and I pulled out all the stops to make it a Christmas none of us would ever forget.

I probably went completely over the top but I didn't care one bit!

The outside of our house was decorated with fairy

lights and model reindeers and I even bought a snow machine and hung it out the back bedroom window so it floated down past the patio doors for the kids!

I hired a foldaway table from a lovely local company as ours wasn't big enough for fifteen and I decorated it with name tags, pine cones I picked up in B&M and crackers I'd bought from Tesco.

I ordered lots of beautiful desserts from Marks & Spencer, little cake stands on eBay for the canapés and I felt like the hostess with the mostest!

Everyone stayed really late having drinks, playing games and singing on the karaoke machine – no one wanted the day to end.

We'd arranged for Jamie's family to stay in a nearby hotel so there was no need for them to rush back to London that night and we did round two the next day when the lads watched the football on the telly while us girls hit the shops to find some bargs in the sales. Total bliss.

I kept on thinking the whole day that it was too good to be true and something was bound to go wrong at any moment (typical me), but it all went to plan and I had a real sense of achievement after it. I actually felt like I was on some *Beauty and the Beast* Disney set. It was so beautiful.

Once everyone had left, me and Jamie actually high-fived each other. It felt like everything we'd been hoping for had come together perfectly for our families.

'Well done, baby!' he said. 'You smashed it!'

And then, not for the first time that year, we collapsed in an exhausted heap on the sofa.

Given the chance, I think we could have both slept for a week.

I think that hosting Christmas for the whole family for the first time is a real coming-of-age moment. I finally felt like a proper grown-up!

For me it was, without doubt, the best Christmas ever and hopefully the first of many just like that . . . although I don't think I could take the pressure of doing it every year!

When we bought this place as a three-bedroomed detached new-build back in July 2016, we chose the corner plot on our cul-de-sac on purpose, with eventually extending it in mind.

We knew the house had huge potential for being 'grown', but having sunk all our savings into the deposit, we were skint and starting from scratch and didn't think we'd be in a position to go ahead with it for several more years.

Both of us feel extremely fortunate that the success of Mrs Hinch meant we were able to achieve our extension goals much sooner than we'd ever dreamed and so last year we decided to go for it. We hired an architect who drew up the plans which we then reworked a little to make it completely perfect for us. He actually came up with the idea of turning the original third bedroom I used as my make-up room into a landing at the top of the stairs which was so clever and not something I'd thought of myself.

It's now one of my favourite spots in the whole house even though Jamie has hilariously nicknamed it 'the waiting area' because I added a chair, rug and a coffee table!

We had this big bit of garden running right around the left-hand side of the house which we never used so it made sense to extend sideways and double our living space. It basically meant building a second house and then joining the two together.

As with any building works, there were various bumps in the road and they were sometimes stressful, but finding ways round them was something we had to get used to and try and keep positive. It's all part of the process and the hardest parts are always the most character-building! That's what we kept telling ourselves, anyway . . .

For instance, our planning permission was turned down at first because the whole thing was apparently too wide and this then put everything back by about five weeks.

By that time I was pregnant with Ronnie and the setback meant there was no chance that the work would have been finished by the time he arrived.

Not ideal, but there's no point in getting in a twist over hiccups like this – you have no choice but to go back to the drawing board and re-work the plans, which is exactly what we did.

And yes, it means the whole thing is half a metre

smaller than we originally wanted . . . but size isn't every-thing, right?! And I'm so grateful we were able to go ahead at all.

As the work progressed I kept it all quiet on Instagram, mainly because I didn't want to alert the media to what was happening. I wasn't deliberately hiding anything from my followers, but the last thing I needed while pregnant and living on a building site was the added stress of the press turning up trying to get a picture of what was going on.

So I tried to keep everything as normal as possible, although I'd always been open about the fact that extending was my dream and I even wrote about it in *Hinch Yourself Happy*. When I listed my goals, I talked about wanting a dining room, a bigger lounge and a fireplace – it's amazing to think I've now got all three. I'm so grateful.

I dropped little hints along the way as well. When I announced I was pregnant, obviously the first thing my Hinchers said was 'Congratulations!' but the second was: 'Oh no, does this mean Henry will lose his room?'

That was the funniest thing, but people were genu-inely really concerned about it.

By that time our extension planning was well on the way, so I put a message on my stories saying: 'Don't worry, Henry won't be losing his room', and I added a picture of a builder with a hammer.

So that was a major clue as to what we had going on and my followers all knew something exciting was happening. My handsomes was never going to be turfed out!

The work really began around April 2019 and we used local builders who were completely amazing. They were always really respectful of our space, which meant we could continue living at home quite comfortably, and they worked round the clock to get it finished so quickly. We've used them before for bits around the house and garden so we trust them; one of the perks of living in a small town and everyone knowing everyone. Some people assumed we didn't even pay for our extension because I shared their construction Insta page on my story. How bonkers is that! We paid full price. I just shared their page because they're fab and that's one of the things I stand for and am so passionate about.

I know a lot of people thought we must have been mad to go ahead with such a big renovation while I was heavily pregnant with Ronnie, but, to be fair, for the most part we weren't majorly disrupted.

They pretty much built the extension as a separate building to the original house and it was just a case of knocking through right at the end.

My unpredictable and irrational pregnancy hormones played havoc on the odd occasion, though, I have to admit. This is really embarrassing and I can't believe I'm about to tell you, but I remember they put a big sheet of chipboard up in our living room to serve as a temporary wall before they properly knocked through. Every bit of work in the new part of the house was going on behind this piece of wood.

Guys, I freaked out when I clapped eyes on it for the first time. I took one look at it and said to Jamie: 'Oh, hell no.'

You could obviously hear a lot of noise coming from the other side of it, but that wasn't the issue.

My issue was that the wood was dark brown and I *hated* it! I didn't want brown in my lounge and it was really upsetting me. Admittedly far more than it should have, but hey, pregnancy does really funny things to you.

I sat down on the sofa but I couldn't even concentrate on the TV because all I could see was this brown chipboard in front of me.

Jamie looked at me helplessly and said: 'What can we do, babe?'

Which is how we, along with one of my friends who had popped over to say hi (and probably immediately regretted it!) ended up spending one evening until midnight painting the woodchip wall white in an attempt to make it look and feel more homely. More Hinched!

I even made Jamie hang a picture on it when it was dry. I kid you not!

The builders must have thought I was insane. When they saw it a few of them looked at me like, 'Are you OK, hun?', and at Jamie as if, 'Is your wife all right?'

But it made me calmer at a stressful time, so in my eyes, it was worth it and it did the job.

And as I'm writing this I've just remembered that I could not cope with the fact that I had a Portaloo on my front lawn for the entire time the building work was taking place. I couldn't mentally wrap my head around it, guys! I don't have any idea how Portaloos work, and I don't think I want to know, but the thought of it being out there on my front grass just bothered me! Like, what happens to everything that gets left in there? All of the . . . yanno? Does it just sit in there overnight to fester? Could the neighbours smell anything? I had to try really hard to resist offering them some Harpic Pine.

As I mentioned earlier, we took off around the countryside for the first six or seven weeks of Ronnie's life while they finished everything off, and it was the best thing we could have done. My dad was on site every day overseeing the work so we knew it was all in good hands and it meant we escaped the worst of the mess and chaos – two things I don't generally handle very well even without a newborn baby to look after!

I must confess, though, it was so strange when we came back, stepping through the door of a home I didn't recognise for the first time.

I was like, 'Whose house is this?'

It was the weirdest feeling being in a place I loved so much but which no longer felt familiar. I almost wanted my old home back! It actually made me burst into tears – how bad is that?!

I felt so ungrateful, but I was still struggling with my

emotions after Ronnie's birth and my hormones were all over the show. I think poor Jamie must have wondered what the hell was going off. It wasn't like they could knock it down and take it all away!

Of course once we'd done the decorating and I was able to add the finishing touches with accessories and furniture, it didn't take long for me to fall in love with it. I'm so very proud of what we've achieved with our home.

No surprises with the décor – I went for my favourite white and greys, so it really was an extension of what we already had. For Ronnie's room we chose pastel blue and white. My rug, TV unit and style of sofa are all the same – why change things you love so much and which still have plenty of life left in them?

I get asked about the layout a lot so I'll try and explain it as best I can. Basically, our original bedroom is now the guest room and Henry obviously still has his 'quarters', so nothing has changed on that side at all.

As I said before, the old third bedroom is now the landing (or waiting area . . .) and across from that are the two new bedrooms, which are ours and Ronnie's.

I know a lot of people expect me to have a walk-in wardrobe with downlights and shoes and bags on display like they're in some sort of museum, but that's not what I'm about. I don't even own enough shoes to display, if I'm honest. I never wear heels because of my height, so what am I supposed to display in the downlighters? Slippers? Ha! If I had a walk-in wardrobe it would have meant

Ronnie's room being smaller, Henry losing his room and us losing our guest room (which will hopefully one day become baby number two's room), so a walk-in wardrobe had no place in our home in my opinion. And I didn't bat an eyelid about it. For now we have everything we need and more.

We had these gorgeous custom wardrobes fitted by Dan from Taylor Bespoke, which look very posh. I love to organise them with my eBayer organisers, mini baskets and even the caddies I use for Ronnie's baby bits. But it made me laugh because I don't really have any clothes to fill them with. Oh well! It's still the case that I get more of a thrill buying cloths than I do clothes. And, if I'm honest, I struggle to find clothes that fit me well. Maybe I'm a bizarre shape? I'm not sure. So I find myself wearing a lot of the same pieces, just in different colours.

I loved putting Ronnie's nursery together, choosing the loveliest accessories like his 4-foot freestanding cuddly giraffe (or Greg as I named him) and his moon and stars ceiling light from eBay and creating a reading corner with a cosy rocking chair and bookshelf.

He didn't actually sleep in there until he was about ten months old because I couldn't bear to take him out of our room before that. I know from your DMs that a lot of you experienced the same feelings with your own babies and it really helped me to hear your stories. I was starting to worry that I was getting it all wrong by keeping him in with me and Jamie for so long and not letting him learn to sleep on his own.

But it just feels like such a big step, doesn't it? Ronnie will always be my baby and for a long time I just wasn't ready for him to leave us.

If you're in the same boat, please don't ever feel pressured to do anything just because other people voice an opinion on what you and your baby 'should' be doing. Everyone's feelings and circumstances are different and you have to do what makes you and your baby most happy and comfortable. I know that now.

Another thing of joy to come from the work we had done is my amazing loft. As you know, I was going to have a loft ladder fitted but the hatch was too narrow, which was so disappointing.

When we went back to the drawing board, I found the fabulous (and now Insta-famous) Mr Loft Ladder who installed the telescopic ladder which has opened up a whole new beautiful world to me. Literally!

There's a film called *The Hugga Bunch*, which I was absolutely obsessed with when I was younger, and there's a scene in it where the grandmother sits with her granddaughter in the loft with this little light, looking through all the family's old photo albums. It's really stuck with me all these years and to be honest I've pictured myself doing it ever since I first watched the movie.

I always thought that just having a little area to relax and have a think over everything would be so lovely and so I've been making up a memory corner for Ronnie in the loft.

I no longer have to wait for Jamie if I ever need anything from up there. I can pull down my ladder, climb up there all on my own and sit on my upcycled ottoman and look through all our photos. Just thinking about it makes my heart feel happy.

Once the builders all packed up, part of me thought 'Never again.' We breathed a sigh of relief and loved having our home back to ourselves again.

But now I feel like renovations are a bit like childbirth – you forget the pain and before you know it, you're on to planning the next one!

Only a few months after the extension was completed, I started thinking. What if . . .

'Babe,' I said to Jamie one evening and he held his breath, realising I was coming up with another one of my ideas.

'What if we took down the wall between the dining room and the kitchen?'

It would mean I could keep an eye on Ronnie playing while making the dinner, I'd be able to chat to whoever else was in the house and we'd have the natural light flood through the house from the patio doors.

Once I had the idea in my head, I couldn't shake it. I put it on my stories and asked you guys what you thought and the reaction I got in response convinced me I was on to something. Everyone was saying to go for it!

We got some plans drawn up very quickly after that. We got in the car and drove to our most local kitchen showroom just down the hill and sat with a kitchen designer for about four hours. They were amazing! Once we had the designs we called on our builders again (the same guys who did our extension) and Jamie said to them: 'Guys, we've designed a new kitchen. Any way you could fit it?' Of course, they said yes. But then Jamie explained we were off to Disney so was there any way it could be done while we were out of the house (it made so much sense). I didn't think it would be possible with such short notice, but they managed to get 80 per cent of the work completed by the time we got home. How amazing is that! At the time I had a few messages through asking if this was all a set-up to get a free kitchen. Absolutely not! It was a quick spur-of-the-moment decision which came to life and was one of the best moves we've made for the house. And I paid for all of it despite being offered a completely free kitchen.

I was so nervous about getting it done, though. I loved my old kitchen – it's where all of this began and so I had a huge emotional attachment to it. Not only that, but the tiled sink splashback that me and my dad put together meant so much to me – there were so many happy memories wrapped up in that room. Can you believe I still have my original sink on the rafters in the garage because I can't face parting with it? And, of course, I've repurposed the tiles.

I was also scared in case there was a backlash against me from people who had grown used to my old kitchen and wouldn't like the change. I know it sounds daft, but that sink didn't feel like any old sink. Shining it was such a big part of my Hinching routine – our Hinching routine – and I wondered where we'd all be left without it. And the truth is, the company that made our original kitchen cupboards had gone into liquidation so there was no way we could've just added to the existing cupboards; everything had to come out and we had to start from scratch.

I needn't have worried. You guys were just as excited as I was, so it felt like we were all going through it together.

I decided it was my thirtieth birthday present to myself – and we were so lucky that our builders managed to squeeze in the work while we were away.

I remember coming home from the holiday and not really knowing what we'd be faced with. We arrived back late at night and I was terrified opening the front door.

There was a lot of mess! All our kitchen stuff was piled up in the living room under protective sheets, but I didn't care, because the lads had made such great progress and I could see straightaway that we'd made the right decision about the wall. I was so thrilled with my new kitchen.

Jamie immediately called the hole in the wall 'the drive-thru' which really made me laugh and that name has stuck ever since.

I love my drive-thru! It's made it such a sociable, light-filled space and I can't imagine life without it now.

I couldn't wait to host our first dinner party and serve our guests food at the drive-thru!

And the best thing is I can pop round to my mum and dad's and see my old kitchen whenever I like because it was refitted in the little outbuilding in their garden. My dad was over the moon with it and uses it as a workspace where he potters about doing DIY and fixing things, bless him. And he's going to use his new outdoor kitchen when we all have our big family BBQ get-togethers in the future. I can't wait.

When I go round there I always like to pop out and give the worktops a wipe-down and rearrange the cupboards, just for old times' sake. All the best, Soph.

My dad is so happy out there – that's where he spent most of the lockdown, actually – and it's all worth it just for that.

I think the fact we missed out on using the garden for so much of last summer because of the building work made me determined to make the most of it this year. I'm rarely happier than when I'm sat in the egg chair on a sunny day with a cup of tea, watching Ronnie play on the lawn.

Our garden gets the sun all day long and I was so thankful we had all that outdoor space.

I've been adding bits to the garden all year and I'm so chuffed with my Spiralites, which I found on eBay, and the solar lanterns I got from B&M. They light up the garden at night and make it look so twinkly and pretty.

I'm also really pleased with my potting table, which

was another idea I had that made Jamie think I'd lost it, especially when I asked him to fix my old IKEA rail from the kitchen to the wall so I had somewhere to hang my gardening gloves.

I love finding new homes and uses for things. Like the tiles from my old kitchen splashback, which I smashed up and set in concrete and are now stepping stones that my big garden pots sit on. And the IKEA unit I had in the old kitchen, which is now the cute little BBQ station I had so much fun putting together earlier this year.

I don't like to waste anything, and so if I can repurpose something I will do it. And I love that the tiles which hold so much sentimental value to me will continue to live on in our home.

To anyone thinking of doing some renovation work, I'd tell you to follow your heart and just go for it. If I managed it with a newborn, so can you!

The mess isn't forever, so push through it and focus on how fantastic it's going to be at the end.

I think getting away during the worst of the building work was key for us and I'd definitely recommend it to anyone in the same position. Even just a week in a caravan park or an Airbnb would help, because it can be very stressful and the noise isn't great for anyone who suffers with their nerves. A bit of separation from the dust and chaos is never a bad thing.

You know, the funny thing about taking on a big project is that just at the point where you feel like you're a million miles away from the finish and you're not sure how much more you can stand, suddenly everything comes together really quickly. Everyone told me that at the time – I didn't believe them but it's true.

Communication and staying on good terms with our neighbours really helped as well. We love our street and were already very friendly with the people around us and they were so supportive of all our plans, then we kept them up to date all through the process.

We had our driveway extended as part of the build and offered to stretch it all the way across to our opposite neighbours as a way of saying thank you for putting up with all of the madness. They were delighted with that because it meant they gained an extra car parking space which they use every day.

It was the least we could do for them having had to live with our mess and noise out the front for quite a while.

As for what's next, we're thinking we might get panelling done throughout the hallway and up the stairs and on the landing, because I think that looks so luxurious. I would love to have it done. I've been looking on Instagram and getting inspo!

And we'd maybe like to get a little sunroom built just off the lounge so Ronnie can have a playroom looking out on to the garden.

But those are things for the future – I have to leave it for now because me and Jamie both need a break from renovation work. As much as I love my builders, I wasn't half pleased to see the back of them for a while.

People ask if there is anything I would have done differently and I can honestly say there isn't. Everything worked out for the best in the end and it was definitely worth all the stress, sweat and tears (um, mainly mine!).

I think more than anything, it's proved to me that you should never stop believing, because you can pull off your dreams. I sometimes look back on my grid at my Christmas dinner table and it still makes me feel a bit shocked, but in a good way. We did that!

This whole Hinching journey has had so many incredible personal moments, but that Christmas Day with the family in our old/new home was definitely one of the most magical so far.

# Twelve

# A Drop into my DMs

I can't say it enough – I love you guys! One of the things I would love to do in the not-so-distant future is get us all together by hosting a huge open-air Hinch festival with cleaning stands for all my favourite brands, live demos, talks and Q&As and, most importantly, lots of fun. Remember when we said we'd all be waving our Minkys in the air when I went on that Insta live just after we'd hit a hundred thousand followers? I'd like to make that dream a reality.

Of course it would be family-friendly with lots to do for the kids, we'd have it in a big field and it would be somewhere we could all finally meet each other. How amazing would that be? Hinch Fest – watch this space!

Having that many of us all together in one place would also give me the chance to chat to lots of you face-to-face and get to know you even better.

Because honestly, one of my favourite things to do at the end of each day and whenever I've got a spare ten minutes is to sit on my sofa and scroll through the DMs you've sent me, read them all and reply to as many as I can. There are lots of them!

I get so many questions about my life and requests for Hinching tips as well as loads of messages of love and support; telling me to keep going and sharing your own experiences of things like being a mummy or a carer, how you cope with anxiety and how you feel about your own body.

No matter what kind of day I've had, they never fail to cheer me up. It's like having 3 million pen pals and I only wish that I could reply to each and every one of you individually.

I do manage to get back to loads, but there are just so many that even if I sat there for a week doing nothing but replying to DMs, I'd still have only scratched the surface. It's something that I really struggle with, actually. Purely because of the guilt I feel thinking, what if someone has messaged me because they need me, and I haven't seen it?

So I thought it would be a good idea to collect together some of the most popular questions I get asked in my DMs and answer them here. Hopefully you'll spot one of yours in the mix!

**Q: What does Jamie really think of all this?**
A: Jamie is more than fine. Apart from the horrible comments and messages I receive and how those affect me, he's loving life. Nothing's changed in Jamie's eyes, we're the same people and like I said before, absolutely nothing

fazes him. He takes it all in his stride so he's the best person I could wish to have by my side.

He's the level-headed one of the two of us and he helps me see things in a different light, which is often very much needed!

**Q: Please get your own TV show! Would you ever do this? Or would you consider doing something like *Strictly* or joining *Loose Women*?**

A: Haha! *At Home with the Hinchliffes* – could you imagine? To tell you the truth, we've been asked to do something like that but I've politely declined. I think the idea sounds quite fun but there's a big difference between putting my stories up and having a camera crew full-time in my home. I think that would be way too much for us.

It would be my mum's absolute dream for me to go on *Strictly Come Dancing*, but it involves a lot of hours of training and I'm not ready to be away from Ronnie for that long. I would also worry that there wouldn't be a professional dance partner tall enough for me and that no one would be able to lift me up! I told you, I worry about everything even if it isn't yet a thing. And dancing live on TV every week means it's going to go wrong at some point, surely, so I'm not convinced my nerves could take it.

So that's where my head is at with *Strictly*. Who knows, though. I'd never say never to most things, so maybe one day you'll see me on that ballroom floor!

And *Loose Women*? I'm not sure, you know. I was offered a regular slot on *This Morning* for cleaning tips but I turned it down because the fear in my stomach having to talk on live TV is on another level. I'd make myself ill if I had to do that every week!

**Q: What are your top five cleaning products?**
A: Can I be greedy and have six?

*Zoflora (any scent, but Springtime is the ultimate for me)
*Flash Bicarbonate of Soda Spray (a new fave of mine, but I can't get enough)
*Astonish Window and Glass Cleaner Spray
*Dr Beckmann's Carpet Stain Remover
*Febreze
*Mr Sheen Multi Surface Polish

Those guys are my Hinching must-haves! Obviously there are plenty of others, too, but I've been really strict with myself.

**Q: What do you love and hate most about being on Instagram?**
A: I love the support and the feeling of finally having somewhere to fit in. Somewhere to belong. I love reading and chatting to you all on DMs and the laughs we have together. I love feeling like I'm part of this community

of amazing people and I love scrolling through other accounts and feeling inspired every day.

The thing I find the most difficult about Instagram is the bullying and the trolling and the pressure I put on myself to try and keep up with the next big thing. Having Ronnie to look after means I don't have the time I'd like to follow trends or watch what everyone else is doing. And actually, even when I did have the time, I've always just done my own thing. My stories are what they are and I'm lucky that you guys seem to love them, so I must be doing something right. You'll notice every so often that I will have a go at new ways of filming or putting my stories together, or maybe even small things like just changing the type styles I use, but that's as technical as it gets around here, guys.

**Q: Does Ronnie ever cry? He always looks so happy!**
A: God, yes, he cries! He shouts, actually. He definitely knows how to use his lungs and tell us what it is he wants (or doesn't want!). I love that he's got that bit of fight in him and has a voice, it'll get him a long way in life.

But basically, he's a very happy boy, very content and he likes to take everything in around him. We're so blessed.

**Q: What breed is Henry and how did you go about finding a good breeder?**
A: Henry is a Golden Show Cocker Spaniel. I found his breeder on a website called pets4homes.co.uk and we went to visit him from there. It's really important to do

your research when buying a dog to make sure the breeder is a legitimate one and the puppy you're buying is happy and healthy. The RSPCA have good advice around this on their website.

I think if we were ever to get another dog we'd get a rescue one next time. But it's not on the cards just yet – we'll have another baby before we get another dog!

**Q: Who are your favourite people to follow on Instagram?**
A: Ahh, I absolutely love @cleaning_with_mario – he is absolutely brilliant and doing so well! I'm so happy for him. He deserves it! He's lovely! Definitely one of life's good eggs.

@walktheearthwriter writes so many beautiful, uplifting quotes and she keeps me feeling really positive. I love her work.

You obviously cannot beat the amazing @mariekondo (what a queen!) and I also love @lauren_dungey who is a body-positive blogger and she helps me feel more confident. She's curvy and she shows herself exactly as she is and I really love that. She makes me think: 'Go on, girl!' Love her!

**Q: What would be your dream holiday?**
A: I spent a lot of time dreaming about holidays while we were in lockdown, as I'm sure a lot of you guys did too. We'd definitely like to explore more of the UK for

sure, but one thing I would absolutely love to do one day is go on a safari with Ronnie and Jamie, maybe to South Africa. I really want to see those incredible animals in the wild. So we'll definitely add that to our vision board.

**Q: What's it like being famous?**
A: Oh, cringe! I don't even like the word famous! I'd call it being in the public eye more than famous, and I think I've said a few times that it's not something I'll ever feel entirely comfortable with. But there are upsides and downsides. The support I get from my followers is second to none and I keep hold of that.

But if I could carry on doing what I'm doing and take away the being in the public eye part, then I would. My experience of 'fame' generally hasn't been fun.

**Q: What do your family and friends think about your fame?**
A: Well, they worry about me a lot more these days, that's for sure, but we don't really talk too much about Mrs Hinch. Nothing's changed in that sense. This has all happened in a really weird way and they don't see me as Mrs Hinch; they just see me as Soph.

Having that normality around me is really important to me.

My mum worries the most. She checks in on me every day.

**Q: Do you still do hairdressing and did you get fully qualified?**

A: For me, Instagram is a full-time job, especially when you add Ronnie to the mix, so there's no spare time for hairdressing these days. But yes, I am fully qualified with my Level 3 which I did through a college and I really enjoyed it. I'm glad I did it.

I thought hairdressing was what my life would be, but to be honest I never had a huge client base and mostly just did family and friends, mainly because I'd constantly worry that someone wouldn't like their hair. I used to sweat to the point I was a nervous wreck! Why can I never do anything without worrying? It's actually really frustrating.

Also, because of my blood condition I can't stand in one place for too long and sometimes with extensions and colouring you're on your feet for hours on end, so I'm not sure how long I would have been able to manage carrying on with hairdressing.

It's lucky that Instagram happened when it did, otherwise I'm not sure what I would have done.

**Q: Where do you buy your clothes from?**

A: I get asked this all the time, which is funny to me because I certainly don't see myself as someone who has any idea what they're doing fashion-wise! I wear a lot of baggy jumpers and off-the-shoulder numbers and lounge sets which I buy from online stores that have tall ranges. It can be very difficult to find clothes for tall girls on the high street.

So I get a lot from In the Style, Missguided, Missy Empire and MissPap – websites like that where I can go to the drop-down box and search specifically for the tall section. It makes life much easier.

I love eBay as well. I get a lot of swing dresses and oversized stuff from there.

**Q: With a busy life of work and kids, my house is a mess! How do I fit cleaning into my already jam-packed schedule?**
A: Gosh, I totally understand that it can be really hard and that having to deal with it all at once can feel very overwhelming. Please don't feel bad about it; you are doing a brilliant job and there are certainly more important things in life than having a clean and tidy house.

I find having my Hinch List is a lifesaver. If it's written down, I know I'll get round to it eventually and it really doesn't matter when. The fear of everything piling up can seem scary, but when you have your list, it's always there and even if it's one thing being ticked off a night, that's an achievement.

So I'd say just aim for little and often, don't put pressure on yourself, do your Hinch List and, most importantly, enjoy it. Finding your favourite products and scents and those cloths which work best for you is the key to enjoying it. I love having a basket full of products and tools that basically do the work for you.

**Q: How do you choose the music to go with your Hinching stories?**

A: Good question! I do have a system in place for this – it's not a case of whacking any old track to any old story. I've actually got a special Hinch List of tracks in the notes on my phone and always refer back to that before I upload a story if it needs a song.

Me and Jamie have a huge mix of music we love, my dad is a big music lover too and my friends are all into R&B. So between us, we've got this! My friends will text me and say: 'Soph, you've got to listen to this song!' and so then I'll add it to my notes section on my phone and I'll make sure it gets used at some point.

I'm also constantly Shazaming songs when I hear them. I can't even walk through a supermarket without thinking, 'This would be a good story song!' and then I'll add it to my notes for next time.

**Q: You should take more time off, Soph! Why don't you? Everyone deserves a break now and again and you must need one!**

A: Thank you. I know, but I worry that people will think I'm taking them for granted or that I've got myself to a good place and so now I'm leaving them behind.

I sometimes get the feeling that people need me to keep them motivated (which I actually love) but then again, I do struggle without proper breaks away, and even one day a week off Instagram gives me some much needed time to refresh. I have been trying to take that day and having the time away from social media has helped me a lot.

Some of the days I've taken off I've spent thinking of some new ideas for my account and other days have been spent doing absolutely nothing. No shame! Heaven!

## Q: What are your favourite and least favourite Hinching jobs?

A: Ha! Well, I detest ironing. Does that count as Hinching? It comes under the home umbrella so I think it counts. I use a Russell Hobbs steamer instead which cuts down the time. Or sometimes my mum will do a pile for me if I'm lucky.

And my favourites? Ooh, it's so hard to choose! I'm pretty weird in that sense because I just love everything. I love the vacuum cleaner lines on a freshly hoovered carpet. I love the satisfaction of using the Dishmatic on my hob and then squeegeeing it off.

But if you pushed me to pick just one, I do still really enjoy shining my kitchen sink. That's my first love.

## Q: When did you fall in love with the colour grey and what is it about it that you like so much?

A: I think it came about when we first moved into our house and I was looking at other people's accounts and on Pinterest for interiors inspiration. A lot of the people I followed seemed to be using grey in their homes and there were also these crushed silver velvet sofas which appeared to be everywhere. I fell in love with them.

So I went with the flow and followed those styles. Obviously I didn't invent grey interiors, I just loved them and ran with it.

I think it's a fab colour. It feels so clean and crisp and fresh. Light yet cosy. And I love that it's literally in the middle of black and white, night and day, a mix of the two.

**Q: What is the best way to get stubborn stains out of clothes?**

A: Elbow Grease has always worked well for me just before you pop the item into the washing machine. But the main thing is to have faith in your Dream Team! I've got my Bold 3-in-1 Pods, my Lenor Spring Awakening fabric conditioner and my Lenor In-Wash Scent Booster (and the Fairy Sensitive Snuggly Soft versions for Ronnie) and they generally do the trick so I don't often feel like I need to use strong stain removers.

**Q: Your house is so neat and tidy! What are your best tips for keeping on top of clutter?**

A: It's not always neat and tidy, I promise you that! I would say my stair basket is absolutely key and it means stuff doesn't lie about in random piles around the house waiting to be cleared away. Anything that needs to be put away upstairs gets chucked in the basket and then taken up when me or Jamie have a spare five minutes.

Labelled baskets is another must for me, and also making sure everything has a home. If you don't know where to put something, don't just put it on the side where it will sit and gather dust for weeks – put it in a basket and go through it when you can.

The drawer organisers I bought are brilliant and really help to keep a sense of order in our clothes drawers and wardrobes.

Finally, don't be afraid to have a good clear-out. Be brave! I do a huge one at the end of each year and any items I've not used for a whole year have to go. Use that one-year rule, be honest with yourself and donate them, sell them or get rid of them. Don't keep what you don't need, it's not worth it.

I keep a few items back for Ronnie's memory box and it's fine to hang on to the things that will bring you joy in years to come when you look back, but the rest of it goes to new homes.

## Q: Where do you get your ideas for Ronnie's food?

A: I get a lot of them online, just by googling. I see what we've got in the fridge and type in something like sweet potato, spinach, egg and baby recipe and see what pops up. I mix and match as well, like the other day when I had a recipe which needed broccoli and spring onion but I didn't have them, I used cauliflower and parsley instead. So I like to play about a bit and make them Ron's recipes. I also follow a load of really helpful weaning accounts on Instagram.

I always make sure to share those that I like in case that will help any of my Hinchers in the same boat as me.

The kitchen isn't where my natural skills lie, I have to say, but I'm getting better and I'm enjoying learning. It's also so lovely to watch Ronnie hoover up the food I've made for him myself. He's such a good eater. I feel proud of myself!

I love the Ella's Kitchen site as well, which is full of good recipes and advice and you can pick the age bracket you're cooking for.

**Q: Will Ronnie have his own Instagram account one day like Henry?**
A: No. Definitely not. We want to protect him as much as we can and so I think it would be unfair for us to do that. It wouldn't be right for our family.

If he chooses to do all of that when he's old enough to make his own decision, then that's his choice. God knows what social media will be like when he's that age, but I'll just have to roll with it and hope he has a positive experience with it.

But while it's in my control and while he's little, it won't happen.

**Q: Where are your favourite places to buy Ronnie's clothes? He's always so beautifully dressed!**
A: Ah, thank you so much! Tesco, would you believe! He lived in their baby grows and sleepsuits when he was little. I love the designs and they wash really well.

I also love small boutiques and businesses who make such beautiful things and deserve the recognition.

**Q: Which beauty products do you swear by?**
A: This year, as you probably have seen, I've been using The Ordinary for my skin and I've really liked all their products I've tried so far. I also love the Garnier face masks.

I really rate the ICONIC make-up range and always have done. I still love Estée Lauder's Double Wear for foundation and Maybelline's Age Rewind for concealer. The Skinny Tan products are my go-to for fake tan. Apart from those staples, I like to try different products when I can, and a lot of the time I go with whatever's on offer in the shop!

I like sharing my finds and favourites with you, but make-up is just a bit of fun for me. I'm no expert – Mrs Hinch is not about to become a beauty blog. Trust me on that!

**Q: What is the best thing to get mould out of bathroom grout? It's so annoying!**
A: Isn't it?! I can't recommend Astonish Mould and Mildew Blaster enough. It's the best. It's very strong, so you need to keep your windows open when you use it, but it works every time.

**Q: Have you always used lists in your day-to-day life and why do you love them so much?**

A: Oh, lists are everything to me. At home, at work, everywhere; I've always used them and I can't imagine life without them. I'm not sure how I'd cope! They help me feel like I'm in control and everything is going to be OK.

I'm a very visual person and it's a way I can see where I want to go and what I need to do to get there. I tick things off which I find very satisfying and I can see immediately what I've achieved and what still needs to be done, and it's all very reassuring to me.

I'm so proud that I was able to bring out my own *Little Book of Lists* earlier this year. I hope you guys find them as helpful as I do – I love seeing yours, so please carry on tagging me into your posts and stories.

**Q: What are your top Disneyland tips?**

A: Definitely plan ahead by circling all the rides you want to go on that day and then ticking them off as you go, like a list. It's a great way of making sure you do and see all the things you want to, because it's so easy to get thrown off track once you're inside the park.

Also, be a child! Throw yourself into it and wear the Mickey Mouse ears, put on the glitter, buy the Disney tracksuit – I did all that and I felt amazing. You actually stand out more if you don't, so Disney yourself up!

I'd totally recommend staying in the Disneyland Hotel,

because it's so close to everything so you feel like you're at the heart of it all. Oh, and pack your comfy shoes because you do a hell of a lot of walking.

Have fun! We'll definitely be going back, and I think when Ronnie's older we'd love to go to the one in Florida.

**Q: What do you do to stay in such great shape?**
A: First of all, please trust me when I say that I'm really not in great shape. But I Hinch! I don't run, jog, cycle or do any classes. I do have a skipping rope which I enjoy using in the garden now and again, but apart from that it's cleaning, which I reckon must burn off a lot of calories every day without me even realising.

Who needs expensive gym memberships when you can scrub, sweep, dust and mop and get a clean house at the same time? What's not to love?

**Q: When you go on a Hinch Haul do you set a budget, and what does Jamie think of the stuff you bring back?**
A: I don't set a budget, but I do go to affordable stores so I never spend very much anyway. Everything is a barg! I'm careful, though, and I only buy things I need – I'm the one who watches the money, much more so than Jamie, actually. I know that might surprise a few people!

He laughs at some of the more 'interesting' items I pick up, but I'm proved right about them because we do put everything to good use. He took the mick out of my pig egg cups I picked up in Aldi earlier this year but he's used them a lot!

**Q: If you could go back in time, what advice would you have given yourself ten years ago?**
A: Stop worrying. It'll be OK. I absolutely would not have listened, though.

I actually wish I could tell myself that now and listen! To tell you the truth, if you ask me the same question in ten years' time when I'm forty, you'll probably get the same answer.

**Q: You sound like you can hold a tune! Do you ever wish you'd tried to make it as a singer?**
A: Haha! No, in a word! I love singing and I think my voice is OK, but I could never be a performer. If I could go into a recording studio completely on my own – just me and a microphone – and sing a song for Ronnie to show him how I feel about him, I'd do that. But never anything more.

**Q: What's the biggest gift you've bought for someone else with your success?**
A: I bought Jamie his dream car for his birthday. I shared with you guys on my stories that we were at the dealership on the day. Jamie had us in there for three hours, having a look around and talking to the salesman. He'd built his perfect motor on the screen, but we ended up

leaving without getting anything. That was all part of the surprise! I went back and sorted it all out at a later date. He was like a kid at Christmas when he saw it and it was worth every penny for that reaction. I love being in a position where I'm able to do nice things for friends and family. It's the best feeling.

**Q: What's the best way to get rid of pet hairs and smells?**
A: Febreze for the smells. And Vamoosh Pet Hair Dissolver in the washing machine is fabulous. Not forgetting a rubber body brush, which is the best for getting pet hair out of the sofa. And a window squeegee for your rugs and stairs.

**Q: Is Jamie as clean and tidy as you?**
A: He's tidier than me but I'm cleaner than him, so we meet in the middle and it works! The thing is, I will go into a room and Hinch it all, but then before I've had time to put all the cleaning products away, Jamie will come in and tidy them before I've even had the chance – teamwork!

**Q: You're very close to your mum. What memories do you have of her cleaning and has that influenced you?**
A: God, yes. I remember a lot of Mr Sheen! I remember the smell and it reminds me of the weekends when my mum did most of her cleaning. She also has baskets for everything, so my obsession with that comes from her.

**Q: What do you miss most about your old life?**

A: A lot. Being able to go out and not having to think twice about everything. I miss being someone that people don't recognise and the normality that came with that. Don't get me wrong. Whenever I do meet my Hinchers out, they've always been so lovely, and in that respect, I am very lucky. But I'll get people staring at me across rooms sometimes, and it'll make me a bit paranoid. I forget it's maybe because they're wondering if I am who I am. I just assume I've got something in my teeth, or a mark on my top, or maybe my hair's a mess. Silly things like that.

But I have so much in my new life that I love, so it all balances out.

**Q: What are the best ways you work to combat your anxiety?**

A: Day to day, cuddles are the best, so Ronnie, Jamie and Henry are the people I go to for those. And Hinching, of course! Doing my before and after photos has a very calming effect – I'm not saying that will work for everyone, but it's what works for me.

**Q: What are the biggest challenges of being a mum?**

A: Gosh, this might take a while! I think more than anything, the enormous guilt you feel and can't shake, however hard you try. I'm constantly battling that.

I couldn't love him any more if I tried, but I question myself all the time. Should I be doing this? Should I know the answer to that? Have I done something wrong? Should we have done something differently there? Is this what's best for him?

And worry as well. Worry upon worry! I worry about him getting his little heart broken one day! It's so hard to think he's going to have to be his own person and go through the same tough life experiences we all have to as human beings.

The tiredness is challenging and so are the broken nights of sleep, but this gets easier and you learn to cope with less sleep than you'd normally like. And once Ronnie started sleeping more through the night I felt like a new woman!

So yes, guilt and worry I would say are my biggest challenges, and there is very little you can do about them, unfortunately.

**Q: Would you ever leave Essex?**
A: To be honest, as much as I love where I live, it's less about Essex itself and more about the people I care about. So it completely depends where my family are – if they leave, I'd leave with them. I could live anywhere if I had them with me or at least nearby.

**Q: You talk a lot about women supporting women – why is it important to you?**
A: Because it's tough out there! And we should stick together. We should be a huge network of support for each other. We are strong, we are amazing and yet some

of us choose to pull each other apart. It makes no sense to me, and it also makes me so sad because it really doesn't have to be like that.

Dimming someone else's light doesn't make your own any brighter. If we all helped each other to shine then imagine what we could achieve.

Maybe I'm naive, but that's how I feel. I'll always work to empower other women.

**Q: Who has been the biggest influence on your life?**
A: Ronnie. He's changed everything and my life has a whole new meaning with him in it. It will never be the same. Life seems more beautiful somehow now. My world is so much better because he's here.

Hopefully that's answered some of the more frequently asked questions. Thank you for all of your DMs over the years. Please keep them coming! I love them.

I read as many as I can and I'll always try and answer as many as I'm able to. I just wish there were more hours in the day so I could come back to you all.

# Thirteen

# What's Next?

I think about the future an awful lot, if I'm honest – I'm definitely one of life's planners! And even when I've got a plan to follow, I'm guilty of worrying about things that haven't even happened yet and over-thinking all of the what ifs!

Since the very start of Mrs Hinch, time has just flown by at whirlwind speed. One of my biggest aims over the next few years is to slow things right down, on the social media front, at least.

I expect you'll know that we'd both love more children – at least one more for sure. Maybe another two if we're very lucky. Jamie's got a thing about even numbers so he would quite happily go up to as many as four! Yikes! Can you imagine!

He's not the one who has to go through pregnancy and labour, though, so I'm not so sure about that. But stick with us and we'll see. Stranger things have happened!

I'd love nothing more than to have a house constantly

filled with our kids, their friends and our families so that there are always people around, coming and going. That's what my mum and dad's house is like.

It's never empty, there is always food in the cupboards, tea in the pot and they're never on their own.

It's the warmest and most welcoming of homes, full of life and laughter, and I'd love to have my own version of that wherever me and Jamie end up.

The time we've spent in isolation this year, being forcibly separated from the people we love the most, has made me realise even more just how important this is to me. It's put so much into perspective.

I want to start working my way through the list of activities me and my friends promised we'd do together as part of my thirtieth birthday celebrations. I've got them all written down in a jar and after all this social distancing, we've got a lot of time to make up.

There's nothing extravagant in there. It's things like going for a picnic, doing Go Ape, going bike riding and wave watching with hot chocolate and fish and chips. So we'll get going on some of those soon – I'll let you know how we get on.

I've also spent a lot of time during the Coronavirus lockdown thinking about the places I'd like to visit once the pandemic is over.

Being unable to travel anywhere has given me seriously itchy feet, but funnily enough, I don't dream about jetting off to expensive places like the Caribbean. I find myself getting excited about exploring the UK.

We have so many wonderful places to visit and so much history and stunning countryside right on our doorstep, and we've not come close to making the most of it. I want to discover the Cotswolds, take in the Lake District and get to know my dad's neck of the woods up in the North East.

I would honestly love to hire one of those big motorhomes so the four of us could all go off on the biggest road trip ever. We'd just drive and drive and stop off at the most random places, staying in fields and letting Henry run free.

Jamie thought I'd lost the plot when I came up with this, as he does with a lot of my ideas at first, but forget luxury holidays around the world; a motorhome trip around the UK is genuinely what I would love to do.

We actually went to look at some motorhomes a few months ago and it properly gave me tingles. I could really see us packing everything up and heading off on the open road in our house on wheels, and it made me so excited!

When Jamie saw them himself, he changed his tune from thinking I was mad and admitted that I could be on to something. Well, I am usually right!

What they do with the small space in those things is so clever, we were both really impressed. They've got everything you could possibly need and I can't wait to make our little holiday happen.

The thought of still being able to get my Hinching

done while on the go makes me so happy – just imagine, I could do a Clockwise Clean of the whole place in one go and in no time!

And I'm not going to lie, I've already started thinking about what my motorhome Hinching basket might look like with all my essential favourite items. Tell me to get a life – I don't care because I'm really excited!

One thing I'm certain of is that I'll never move abroad, because I'm too much of a homebody. Actually, perhaps that's another reason why a motorhome holiday is so appealing to me because it means I can always just pack up and drive home at any point.

Maybe a bit further down the line we'll think about buying somewhere abroad which my family can use for holidays.

To be able to say to my mum and dad, 'Go and have yourselves a long weekend in the villa', would be the most amazing feeling ever. It would mean that Jamie, Ronnie and me could always take off for a few days and not worry about where to stay.

Knowing that one day we might be in a position to buy a second home actually blows my mind and I don't treat it lightly at all. What a privilege that would be.

As far as the house goes, I don't see us moving in the foreseeable future. Our guest room (which was our old bedroom) means there's definitely space for another baby if and when one comes along, and what we have is more than big enough for a family of four.

Well, five when you count Henry, who will always have his own room wherever we live and I make no apologies for that!

People ask why we haven't bought somewhere bigger, but I just don't want it. I love my house, it's perfect for us and I'm so happy. I'm close to my family, we love our neighbours and I've so loved getting the place just how I like it. There is only one thing that would ever make me feel like it's necessary to move and that would be if I ever felt uncomfortable or unsafe in my own home. I wouldn't be able to bear the feeling of being trapped. I know we are very easily overlooked here, and we've had our garden fences made higher and even extra security cameras installed for this reason. But at this moment in time, we're very happy here.

So when I eventually step away from Instagram (don't worry, I'm not going anywhere just yet!), we might have to consider moving to a home that hasn't been on show to millions of people around the world. As well as that, it would mark the start of what would be a new chapter for us and the beginning of a different sort of life.

I'd never sell this house, though. How could I? We've all made history in it! I'll keep it in the family as an investment for Ronnie, because I could never part with it – you saw how I managed to 'keep' my old kitchen by giving it to my dad, so you know how sentimental I am.

But there will be a time, not soon, but at some point in the future, when Mrs Hinch hopefully evolves into something else, away from social media.

You know that I always like to be honest with you guys and I feel I owe it to you to explain a bit more about where my head is at and how things will hopefully pan out one day.

Basically, it makes me feel very out of sorts if I don't know where I'm going and what I'm doing – you know that I, quite literally, live my life by lists and those all-important Hinched ticks.

I've always preferred the security of a plan and the feeling of being in control of my own life. But in this type of job that I now find myself in, that's not always possible.

Sure, I might know what's in my diary for the next few weeks – which meetings and appointments I have and the brands I am working with – but in the longer term, it's often very difficult to know where all this is heading, and that sense of the unknown I find quite overwhelming and it was starting to affect me. My team at Gleam have always been so amazing at opening up my eyes to the possibilities of where this could all lead, and setting up a strategy for any avenues I'd like to go down, but ultimately it's always been up to me to decide which road I would like to take.

So a few months ago I sat down with Jamie and my mum and we had a very open and honest chat about where I wanted my journey to go. Where we *all* wanted it to go, really. Because this isn't just about me; it's a road me and my family are all travelling together. It affects us all in different ways and every step of the way has involved big conversations between us about which direction to take.

It wasn't a business discussion. Instead we spoke about my hopes and dreams and balancing them with what was best for both our family and my sanity and, together, we made some decisions and came up with a five-year plan.

Just having that felt like a huge weight had been lifted from my chest and I've been sleeping a lot easier since we sorted it out.

So, how is the future going to shape up? Well, as much as I love doing what I do, I know that there's a shelf-life to Instagram and although I know it might disappoint some of you to read, I hope you understand (especially after reading this book) that I have no intention of over-staying my welcome. Deep down, if I'm honest with myself, I know I'm not strong enough to deal with the negative side of social media forever.

Eventually, I will walk away from it, but rest assured, I'll still pop on and watch people's stories and check in on how everyone is – you won't get rid of me that easily, guys!

I've been given an opportunity here to help build a lovely community for millions of people and I will carry on doing that for years and years to come, even if I'm not necessarily there in Instagram form.

I will always be here with you guys.

But with regards to me being present as much as I

am now, every day, that's not something I'm going to be able to keep up forever. At this rate, I'll burn out I think.

Besides anything else, who knows where Instagram itself will be a few years from now? If this extraordinary, life-changing, difficult year has taught us anything, it's that you never truly know what is around the corner. Life can blow up in an instant.

The whole thing could go down tomorrow and so it makes sense not to have all my eggs in one basket (or egg house – if you know, you know!). It's only right that Jamie and I plan for a future away from the gram.

My main personal ambition, which I've already started to work on, is to build a brand, which I'm hoping, with enough hard work from me, will stand the test of time, even after I've long gone from the public eye.

It's no secret that I've trademarked my name and over the next five years I'd like to establish a Hinch product range, which would be anything home-related – bedding, cushions, home accessories, storage, organising, cleaning, baby stuff, gifts, loungewear – all the things I really love. If I can help people spruce up their homes at a bargain price, then happy days.

I'd love to be able to hand a successful and trusted company down to Ronnie, something that is a family-run business and a very strong brand – and in turn, he might want to pass it on to his children.

I feel like it might be far-fetched, but maybe, just

maybe. You never know unless you try, and I'm a great believer in following your heart and dreaming big.

That is my dream and you have to put in the time and dedication in order to achieve it, so that's exactly what I'm doing. If only you could all see my Pinterest board, guys (honestly, I'm obsessed).

Another thing I would love to maybe do one day, and this one might come as a bit of a surprise to a lot of you, is be on the radio somehow. I don't even know the first place to start with this one, but as I said earlier, I've really enjoyed being interviewed in the past. Can you imagine the two of us headlining our own Mr and Mrs Hinch radio show one day where we could get Hinchers to call in and we could have live chats, we could do Q&As, just be ourselves and play all of our favourite tunes? I think that would be amazing.

All of this is what I'm passionate about, and the thought of making it a reality massively excites me.

I'll be honest, I want to be at home as much as I can with Ronnie and any future children we may have. My mum stayed home when me and my sister were young and that's how I imagined it with my own children. Anything that allows me to be around to do the school runs, to help out on class trips, to take them to after-school activities, to cook them their dinner every evening and tuck them up in bed every night is the ultimate goal for me. And I would be so grateful to be in a position to do this and wouldn't ever take it for granted.

So as time goes on, I will probably start to trust a lot more of the Mrs Hinch work to other people that I'm super close to – Jamie would love to be heavily involved when it comes to building up the company, and my dad is amazing with numbers, so he would help with the financial ins and outs, which go way over my head.

My friends have lots of different talents and they could all bring something to the table as well. It can be a family business in every sense of the word and one that everyone can play a part in if they want to.

I'll always be at the forefront of the decision-making and be hands on with the creative, visual side of things. I'd make sure that whatever we're bringing out is truly mine, from the colour to the design, how it feels, how it looks and the way it works. From start to finish I will be at the head of all of that. I'd never whack my name on something if I hadn't been there from the beginning with it and followed it all the way through.

I know I'm never going to be some cutting-edge businesswoman. I've never been interested in any of that. I'm just me. But what I do seem to have is instinct. I'm like my mum in that sense. Maths, English, Geography and all the rest of it aren't our strong points, but our common sense and gut tell us a hell of a lot.

I reckon you can get through a lot in life with that.

People remind me all the time that this opportunity I've found myself lucky enough to be wrapped up in is a once-in-a-lifetime chance. Some have told me I should take as much from it as I can and go for it; say yes to everything and just let the cash roll in. But I could never and would never do that. All of this means so much more to me, and I have never been motivated by money. But what I am motivated by is reaching those goals I've set for myself and being able to tick off those boxes.

What's most important to me is being true to myself and authentic, and providing content that is absolutely right for the followers I love so much. I want to be someone people know they can trust and who they regard as their friend. Because that is how I feel inside.

I don't want to ever be known as someone who sold their soul to the highest bidder.

Hopefully, showing that I have those morals and that integrity will stand me in good stead for the future when it comes to building a strong, lasting and trustworthy brand. I genuinely care about what I put out into the world.

Having my plan in place and knowing that the future is clearer has had a really positive effect on my mental health and is making me feel a lot happier. The pressure that builds up with a life on social media is not always healthy, and so knowing that it's not forever and having long-term goals mapped out in my head puts me more at ease.

I will know when it's time to call it a day, 100 per cent. Like with everything else, I will listen to my gut instinct.

And wherever I go next, I'm taking you guys with me. I promise you that.

# All the Best

So there you go. That's me. No holds barred!

I said at the start of this book that I was nervous about writing it and revealing so much about myself.

I was scared of writing about the very personal challenges I deal with on a daily basis and the fact that being open about them might seem weak or maybe even show a lack of gratitude for everything I have in my life that's amazing. Because there is so, so much that is. I know just how lucky I am, and I will be forever grateful.

But it's funny, the more I dug into my past and got it all written down, the more comfortable I became with it all. I've been surprised by how therapeutic it's been to put pen to paper and I feel like I've made my peace with a lot of what's happened.

And not only have I found it incredibly healing to get all of this out, I'm also more convinced than ever that this is absolutely the right use of the platform I'm lucky enough to have.

I've been given this amazing opportunity to share my truth and tell you all about the things I've been going through in my life, and hopefully being honest will help people who are going through similar difficulties.

It hasn't felt like a case of exposing weakness. Quite the opposite, actually.

I've found so much strength from opening up, and it's given me back a sense of control and of courage as well as the chance to lay some ghosts to rest.

I think it's important that my followers know that my life hasn't been perfect. I always try to keep my account as positive as I can, because so many of you tell me that you see it as a bit of an escape for you. But so much of what we see on social media doesn't always truly reflect what's actually going on and it often doesn't feel like the right space to share such personal experiences.

This feels right.

Much of the writing process has been like a long trip down memory lane for me – I spoke to my mum a lot about my childhood, which was so lovely and there were many happy times I'd long forgotten that came flooding back to me during our chats.

Digging out the old photo albums was brilliant fun and we had such a laugh as I remembered family holidays, my favourite toys, dodgy haircuts and even dodgier outfits.

I just hope you guys don't judge me on some of the embarrassing snaps I've included in the book! It would be great if you could send me some of your own funny pictures from your childhoods – I'd love to see them. You know where to find me.

I loved writing about Jamie and our first few years together and I'm so pleased you guys will feel like you know a bit more about our story now. It seems so long ago because life is so different now, but it was great to relive those carefree days.

It also reminded me what an amazing source of strength he is for me through all of this, and when I say I couldn't do it without him, I mean it 100 per cent.

It was probably sitting down to write about Ronnie that was the most emotional part of all this. But I knew it would be.

Becoming a mother is the most important thing I'll ever do in my life and my most important job and I very much wanted to do Ronnie justice in this book. I really wanted to get across just how much he has changed our lives for the better, what he has taught us and the overwhelming love I have for our little family.

But I also wanted to be honest about the ups and downs of motherhood. I think it's so important we, as women, feel empowered to share our stories and help other mums and caregivers realise that they are never alone.

I really hope I've been able to do that here.

I also hope that I've managed to make you laugh. Life can be tough, but laughter always helps – it's one of the reasons Jamie and I work so well together, because whatever life throws at us, we eventually see the funny side. The silver lining.

Some days it takes longer than others but we always get there in the end!

More than anything, I hope you come away feeling that you know me even better now. You guys are such an important part of my life – over the last few years I've laughed with you and cried with you, and you have given me more than I could have ever wished for.

So, what I really want to say is, thank you.

Thank you for always sticking by me. Thank you for believing in me. Thank you for the friendship and the laughs. Thank you for giving me your love and support; your kindness and your time.

Thank you for being you. And for allowing me to be me.

All the best, always.

Love Soph xx

# Bonus Chapter: Lennie

Isn't it funny how the moments where you feel happiest are often the most simple and ordinary?

We were on our first holiday as a family of four last autumn, on a campsite in a motorhome, sat under a blow-up gazebo. The weather was chilly, so we were in our winter coats and wrapped up against the cold in big cosy blankets, and I had both my gorgeous boys, Ronnie and Lennie, sitting on my lap.

And I thought: This is it. This is all I've ever really wanted. I know it's so easy for people to spend their lives aiming for the next big thing, worried about what they haven't got and what they still need to achieve.

But what is life about, really and truly? I know the answer to that question is different for everyone. For me, it's about being happy with my family and so that moment felt like it. There was nowhere else I wanted to be – and I've been to the Maldives!

That's not to say, of course, that life has been a bed of roses since Lennie came along.

If I'm honest, it was even more of a shock to my system going from one to two than it was just having Ron. It's been a lot harder than I thought it was going to be.

Getting into a routine with our two boys and working out how on earth to get anything else done has been a struggle. My mum said the Terrible Twos with a newborn is the hardest combination and I so get what she means now! But honestly, I wouldn't change a thing.

I couldn't have wished for a better pregnancy with our Lennie. You'll remember that I had a lot of complications with Ron, on top of the 24/7 nerves.

With Len, it was a whole different ballgame. Yes, I had the same worries everyone else has: Is he OK? Is he moving? But I loved every minute of being pregnant and kept busy by getting his nursery all perfect, which was a real passion project of mine. I hadn't been able to do that for Ron because we were bang in the middle of extending the house when I was expecting.

When we found out we were having another boy, I was over the moon. I was happy to have a little baby boy or a little baby girl. Baby being healthy is what matters most. But if I could have chosen, I would have said another boy because I really wanted Ron to have a brother.

A lot of people said: 'Oh I bet you're disappointed you're not having a girl!' which made me smile because I am genuinely so happy we've got our Hinch bros. I think a lot of people hope for one of each, maybe? But I couldn't be more thrilled.

If the pregnancy was smooth though, the birth was anything but.

Our NHS is amazing, but it was a scary experience for me and, in fact, it all happened so fast that I didn't even make it to the labour ward. I ended up giving birth in a tiny side room in the reception area. I thought Jamie was going to miss Lennie being born and he very nearly did, to be fair. But he was allowed in for the last ten minutes.

I really wanted him in there with me all the time, but because of the pressures of the pandemic he couldn't be. Which I completely understand, of course, and I know we're all going through it together, but it doesn't make it any easier.

I had no pain relief (no time for that!) so had to do my best to breathe through it, making use of the gas and air. I remember at one point I'd inhaled quite a bit and must have looked spun out. Jamie couldn't help but laugh.

He said: 'Soph, are you OK? Are you with it?'

I was like: 'Er no, not really.'

And then it was over almost as soon as it had started and we had our second beautiful baby. We had Lennie.

Born on 22 May 2021 and weighing in at 7lb 4oz, our boy.

I've been open with you in this book about just how tough I found the early days of being a mummy the first time round and so I was determined to try some things differently this time, having learnt what works best with Ron.

While I was pregnant with Lennie, I made a list of what I would have changed if I could, and what it boiled down to was giving myself some more time to adjust. I needed to just stop and focus on baby and that meant having a complete break from everything else.

The pandemic stopped all the visitors you normally get, which meant I wasn't seeing anyone outside our bubble and that actually helped me in a way because I didn't get that feeling of being overwhelmed, if that makes sense.

Of course, a massive part of you wants to show off your lovely baby but it's such a full-on time. My little bit of advice to new mums is to take your time and don't feel bad for doing absolutely nothing other than being with your baby.

It's OK to say: 'Not today. Maybe tomorrow.' And if tomorrow is still too soon, it's fine to say: 'Not yet. Another time.'

With Ron, I was trying to fit everyone in as soon as I could and feeling bad that he was a week old, and people hadn't seen him. But really, I would have benefitted from telling people: 'Not yet.'

I took nearly four months maternity leave with Lennie in the end, which I know isn't very much compared to some, but for me it felt like a godsend. I checked in with my followers now and again, but I limited how much work I was involved in behind the scenes and was very strict about the times I'd work, so I was able to really switch off and it made the first few months a totally different experience.

It makes me feel a bit guilty, if I'm honest, because I didn't do that with Ron and I really wish I had, but things don't always work, do they?

You can't change the past; you can only focus on the here and now and this time I made the necessary changes and was able to really enjoy just being Mum.

When you work for yourself, it can be scary opting out like that and there was part of me thinking that when I came back, everyone might be gone. But you know what? There were actually more of you there than when I left! That is something I will never get my head around but will always be so grateful for.

My followers were even messaging me and telling me: 'Soph, don't come back until you're ready. Take your time. We miss you but enjoy this time.' And they were so right. It was the best thing to do.

I also managed to breastfeed for longer this time, which I was really pleased about. I think it had a lot to do with the fact I had to stay in hospital for two nights after the birth – when you're on antidepressants they have to monitor baby, just to make sure there's no withdrawal or any other issues.

But it was a blessing in disguise because it was just me and Lennie, and having the support of the amazing nurses was just incredible. They showed me how to get him to latch properly and it was a whole new experience for me.

When I had Ron, I gave birth at 4 a.m., left at 1 p.m., went home and was like: 'What the hell do I do now?!'

So having those extra couple of nights was a real bonding time for us. Those midwives and nurses really know what they're doing, and we got such a head start thanks to their knowledge, care and time.

I walked out of that hospital really feeling like I'd got this. I knew what Lennie needed and I'd kept him happy and fed for two days completely on my own and I had this real sense of achievement from that.

As a second-time mum, I've got a bit more confidence through all the challenges. Having said that, you're always chasing your tail and what worked yesterday and for one baby, might not work today and probably won't tomorrow either.

You never really know the score, do you? But that's OK, we do our best and we make it through. The whole thing is such a constant learning experience!

I've been much better at asking for help this time round. I've been to the GP a few times and I've switched my antidepressants recently because the one I was on during pregnancy and breastfeeding just wasn't working out for me. My levels still aren't quite right, but I'm trying to settle myself and find my way. I know I'll get there.

Jamie has been much more understanding of my

hormones this time and he knows that if I randomly start crying not to be alarmed! I'm just a new mum going through the new mum ups and downs. He's not been perfect, and sometimes I've still wanted to rip his head off, but he's been brilliant, really.

And Henry? Poor Henry. When we came home with Lennie, he looked at me as if to say: 'Oh Mum, not another one!' But he just adapts to everything.

When the boys are asleep, me and Henry cuddle up on the sofa and it's one of my favourite parts of the day. I will never leave Henry out. I might not be able to give him my full, undivided, nonstop attention anymore, but I make sure I put him to bed every night without fail and I talk to him all the time. He knows exactly how loved he is.

He is my stress-reliever and my go-to for any form of anxiety, worry or panic. If I need to shut the door for five minutes to get away from everything, I take Henry with me – I can't explain how much of an important part of my life he is. I don't know what I'd do without him.

Lennie, like Ron, is obsessed with Henry. He looks out for him all the time and as soon as he catches sight of him, the biggest smile appears across his little face. He's like that with my sister's dogs too. I just know he's going to be such a big dog lover like the rest of us.

I'm excited for the future. I can't wait to watch our boys grow up to be best friends. Ron is the best big brother to Lennie and has already started showing him the ropes. Maybe, if we're lucky, there will be another little one in the mix at some point. We definitely want a third, 100 per cent.

I want to have more motorhome holidays, where it doesn't matter if it rains or the toilet leaks or you lose all the water because someone accidentally left the tap running.

None of that matters, as long as you're together. That, for me, is true happiness.

# Acknowledgements

I'd like to start off by saying thank you so much to my family for being there and supporting me through this crazy roller coaster of a journey that none of us ever saw coming.

To my husband Jamie, without you, none of this would be possible. You are my best friend and there isn't anyone in the world I'd rather have by my side through all of this. I love you more than I could ever tell you with words and we make the best team.

My darling Ronnie, you are the piece of our puzzle that we never even knew was missing. I've never known a love like the love I feel for you every moment of every day, and everything I do is for you, my boy. You are my whole world and you make me so proud.

Henry, I know you have absolutely no clue what's going on here boy, but I need to tell you this: no matter how I'm feeling, when you come up to me and bury your head under my chin wagging your tail, I instantly forget any of my worries. For those few minutes everything in the world feels right again. I love you, Handsomes, more than you'll ever understand.

Mum, I will never find enough words to tell you just how much you mean to me. You were my first best friend, you're still my best friend today and my absolute rock. Thank you for always reminding me that my best is always enough.

Dad, you've taught me to work hard and to keep going even on those tough days. I know where you started in life, and I know that's something you've never forgotten. I too will forever remember to think in this way. So thank you for teaching me to stay grounded and always remember who I am.

Sam, I was completely obsessed with you growing up, have looked up to you my whole life and still continue to do so even now. I always will. You have no idea how proud I am of the woman you are; so strong, so loyal and so brave. As long as we have each other, we will always be OK. My big sister, I love you.

I also want to thank my incredible publishing team at Penguin. To my editors Fenella and Charlotte; to my literary agent Abigail; and to Joey and Beth, who all helped me tell my story and bring my thoughts to life on the page.

And finally, but most importantly, I want to thank you, my Hinchers. Without you, none of this would be a reality and I can't even begin to tell you how grateful I am. I feel so incredibly blessed and overwhelmed by the love and support I feel from you every single day. I'm so proud of this community we've built, and I just know that through it all we've made life-long friends. You've helped me to believe in myself, love me for me (exactly as I am) and feel proud of myself. And for that, and for everything, I will forever be thankful.

# He just wanted a decent book to read ...

Not too much to ask, is it? It was in 1935 when Allen Lane, Managing Director of Bodley Head Publishers, stood on a platform at Exeter railway station looking for something good to read on his journey back to London. His choice was limited to popular magazines and poor-quality paperbacks – the same choice faced every day by the vast majority of readers, few of whom could afford hardbacks. Lane's disappointment and subsequent anger at the range of books generally available led him to found a company – and change the world.

*'We believed in the existence in this country of a vast reading public for intelligent books at a low price, and staked everything on it'*
**Sir Allen Lane, 1902–1970, founder of Penguin Books**

The quality paperback had arrived – and not just in bookshops. Lane was adamant that his Penguins should appear in chain stores and tobacconists, and should cost no more than a packet of cigarettes.

Reading habits (and cigarette prices) have changed since 1935, but Penguin still believes in publishing the best books for everybody to enjoy. We still believe that good design costs no more than bad design, and we still believe that quality books published passionately and responsibly make the world a better place.

So wherever you see the little bird – whether it's on a piece of prize-winning literary fiction or a celebrity autobiography, political tour de force or historical masterpiece, a serial-killer thriller, reference book, world classic or a piece of pure escapism – you can bet that it represents the very best that the genre has to offer.

## Whatever you like to read – trust Penguin.